Reader's Digest

Rice, Beans & Grains

D0334476

Published by The Reader's Digest Association Limited
London • New York • Sydney • Montreal

Rice, Beans and Grains is part of a series of cookery books called **Eat Well Live Well** and was created by Amazon Publishing Limited.

Series Editor *Norma MacMillan*
Volume Editors *Felicity Jackson, Jane Middleton*
Art Director *Ruth Prentice*
Photographic Direction *Ruth Prentice, Alison Shackleton*
DTP *Peter Howard*
Editorial Assistants *Jasmine Brown, Elizabeth Woodland*
Nutritionist *Jane Griffin, BSc (Nutri.), SRD*

Contributors
Writers *Catherine Atkinson, Anna Brandenburger, Sara Buenfeld, Linda Collister, Christine France, Maggie Pannell, Anne Sheasby, Judith Wills*
Recipe Testers *Catherine Atkinson, Juliet Barker, Anna Brandenburger, Christine France, Emma-Lee Gow, Jane Middleton, Maggie Pannell, Anne Sheasby, Gina Steer, Susanna Tee*
Photographers *Martin Brigdale, Gus Filgate, William Lingwood*
Stylist *Helen Trent*
Home Economists *Julz Beresford, Joss Herd, Bridget Sargeson, Linda Tubby, Sunil Vijayakar*

For Reader's Digest
Project Editor *Rachel Warren Chadd*
Project Art Editor *Louise Turpin*
Production Controllers *Kathy Brown, Jane Holyer*

Reader's Digest General Books
Editorial Director *Cortina Butler*
Art Director *Nick Clark*
Series Editor *Christine Noble*

First Edition Copyright © 2001
The Reader's Digest Association Limited
11 Westferry Circus, Canary Wharf, London E14 4HE
www.readersdigest.co.uk

Paperback edition 2004
Paperback Art Editor *Jane McKenna*

ISBN 0 276 42889 7

Notes for the reader
• Use all metric or all imperial measures when preparing a recipe, as the two sets of measurements are not exact equivalents.
• Recipes were tested using metric measures and conventional (not fan-assisted) ovens. Medium eggs were used, unless otherwise specified.
• Can sizes are approximate, as weights can vary slightly according to the manufacturer.
• Preparation and cooking times are only intended as a guide.

The nutritional information in this book is for reference only.
The editors urge anyone with continuing medical problems or symptoms to consult a doctor.

Contents

6 Introduction

Eating well to live well

8 Versatile Rice, Beans and Grains

30 Soups and Starters

Eating well to live well

Eating a healthy diet can help you look good, feel great and have lots of energy. Nutrition fads come and go, but the simple keys to eating well remain the same: enjoy a variety of food – no single food contains all the vitamins, minerals, fibre and other essential components you need for health and vitality – and get the balance right by looking at the proportions of the different foods you eat. Add some regular exercise too – at least 30 minutes a day, 3 times a week – and you'll be helping yourself to live well and make the most of your true potential.

Getting it into proportion

Current guidelines are that most people in the UK should eat more starchy foods, more fruit and vegetables, and less fat, meat products and sugary foods. It is almost impossible to give exact amounts that you should eat, as every single person's requirements vary, depending on size, age and the amount of energy expended during the day. However, nutrition experts have suggested an ideal balance of the different foods that provide us with energy (calories) and the nutrients needed for health. The number of daily portions of each of the food groups will vary from person to person – for example, an active teenager might need to eat up to 14 portions of starchy carbohydrates every day, whereas a sedentary adult would only require 6 or 7 portions – but the proportions of the food groups in relation to each other should ideally stay the same.

More detailed explanations of food groups and nutritional terms can be found on pages 156–158, together with brief guidelines on amounts which can be used in conjunction with the nutritional analyses of the recipes. A simple way to get the balance right, however, is to imagine a daily 'plate' divided into the different food groups. On the imaginary 'plate', starchy carbohydrates fill at least one-third of the space, thus constituting the main part of your meals. Fruit and vegetables fill the same amount of space. The remaining third of the 'plate' is divided mainly between protein foods and dairy foods, with just a little space allowed for foods containing fat and sugar. These are the proportions to aim for.

It isn't essential to eat the ideal proportions on the 'plate' at every meal, or even every day – balancing them over a week or two is just as good. The healthiest diet for you and your family is one that is generally balanced and sustainable in the long term.

Our daily plate

Starchy carbohydrate foods: eat 6–14 portions a day
At least 50% of the calories in a healthy diet should come from carbohydrates, and most of that from starchy foods – bread, potatoes and other starchy vegetables, pasta, rice and cereals. For most people in the UK this means doubling current intake. Starchy carbohydrates are the best foods for energy. They also provide protein and essential vitamins and minerals, particularly those from the B group. Eat a variety of starchy foods, choosing wholemeal or wholegrain types whenever possible, because the fibre they contain helps to prevent constipation, bowel disease, heart disease and other health problems.
What is a portion of starchy foods?
Some examples are: 3 tbsp breakfast cereal • 2 tbsp muesli • 1 slice of bread or toast • 1 bread roll, bap or bun • 1 small pitta bread, naan bread or chapatti • 3 crackers or crispbreads • 1 medium-sized potato • 1 medium-sized plantain or small sweet potato • 2 heaped tbsp boiled rice • 2 heaped tbsp boiled pasta.

Fruit and vegetables: eat at least 5 portions a day
Nutrition experts are unanimous that we would all benefit from eating more fruit and vegetables each day – a total of at least 400 g (14 oz) of fruit and vegetables (edible part) is the target. Fruit and vegetables provide vitamin C for immunity and healing, and other 'antioxidant' vitamins and minerals for protection against cardiovascular disease and cancer. They also offer several 'phytochemicals' that help protect against cancer, and B vitamins, especially folate, which is important for women planning a pregnancy, to prevent birth defects. All of these, plus other nutrients, work together to boost well-being.

Antioxidant nutrients (e.g. vitamins C and beta-carotene, which are mainly derived from fruit and vegetables) and vitamin E help to prevent harmful free radicals in the body initiating or accelerating cancer, heart disease, cataracts, arthritis, general ageing, sun damage to skin, and damage to sperm. Free radicals occur naturally as a by-product of normal cell function, but are also caused by pollutants such as tobacco smoke and over-exposure to sunlight.
What is a portion of fruit or vegetables?
Some examples are: 1 medium-sized portion of vegetables or salad • 1 medium-sized piece of fresh fruit • 6 tbsp (about 140 g/5 oz) stewed or canned fruit • 1 small glass (100 ml/3½ fl oz) fruit juice.

Dairy foods: eat 2–3 portions a day
Dairy foods, such as milk, cheese, yogurt and fromage frais, are the best source of calcium for strong bones and teeth, and important for the nervous system. They also provide some protein for growth and repair, vitamin B_{12}, and vitamin A for healthy eyes. They are particularly valuable foods for young children, who need full-fat versions at least up to age 2. Dairy foods are also especially important for adolescent girls to prevent the development of osteoporosis later in life, and for women throughout life generally.

To limit fat intake, wherever possible adults should choose lower-fat dairy foods, such as semi-skimmed milk and low-fat yogurt.
What is a portion of dairy foods?
Some examples are: 1 medium-sized glass (200 ml/7 fl oz) milk • 1 matchbox-sized piece (40 g/1½ oz) Cheddar cheese • 1 small pot of yogurt • 125 g (4½ oz) cottage cheese or fromage frais.

Protein foods: eat 2–4 portions a day

Lean meat, fish, eggs and vegetarian alternatives provide protein for growth and cell repair, as well as iron to prevent anaemia. Meat also provides B vitamins for healthy nerves and digestion, especially vitamin B_{12}, and zinc for growth and healthy bones and skin. Only moderate amounts of these protein-rich foods are required. An adult woman needs about 45 g of protein a day and an adult man 55 g, which constitutes about 11% of a day's calories. This is less than the current average intake. For optimum health, we need to eat some protein every day.

What is a portion of protein-rich food?

Some examples are: 3 slices (85–100 g/3–3½ oz) of roast beef, pork, ham, lamb or chicken • about 100 g (3½ oz) grilled offal • 115–140 g (4–5 oz) cooked fillet of white or oily fish (not fried in batter) • 3 fish fingers • 2 eggs (up to 7 a week) • about 140 g/5 oz baked beans • 60 g (2¼ oz) nuts, peanut butter or other nut products.

Foods containing fat: 1–5 portions a day

Unlike fruit, vegetables and starchy carbohydrates, which can be eaten in abundance, fatty foods should not exceed 33% of the day's calories in a balanced diet, and only 10% of this should be from saturated fat. This quantity of fat may seem a lot, but it isn't – fat contains more than twice as many calories per gram as either carbohydrate or protein.

Overconsumption of fat is a major cause of weight and health problems. A healthy diet must contain a certain amount of fat to provide fat-soluble vitamins and essential fatty acids, needed for the development and function of the brain, eyes and nervous system, but we only need a small amount each day – just 25 g is required, which is much less than we consume in our Western diet. The current recommendations from the Department of Health are a maximum of 71 g fat (of this, 21.5 g saturated) for women each day and 93.5 g fat (28.5 g saturated) for men. The best sources of the essential fatty acids are natural fish oils and pure vegetable oils.

What is a portion of fatty foods?

Some examples are: 1 tsp butter or margarine • 2 tsp low-fat spread • 1 tsp cooking oil • 1 tbsp mayonnaise or vinaigrette (salad dressing) • 1 tbsp cream • 1 individual packet of crisps.

Foods containing sugar: 0–2 portions a day

Although many foods naturally contain sugars (e.g. fruit contains fructose, milk lactose), health experts recommend that we limit 'added' sugars. Added sugars, such as table sugar, provide only calories – they contain no vitamins, minerals or fibre to contribute to health, and it is not necessary to eat them at all. But, as the old adage goes, 'a little of what you fancy does you good' and sugar is no exception. Denial of foods, or using them as rewards or punishment, is not a healthy attitude to eating, and can lead to cravings, binges and yo-yo dieting. Sweet foods are a pleasurable part of a well-balanced diet, but added sugars should account for no more than 11% of the total daily carbohydrate intake.

In assessing how much sugar you consume, don't forget that it is a major ingredient of many processed and ready-prepared foods.

What is a portion of sugary foods?

Some examples are: 3 tsp sugar • 1 heaped tsp jam or honey • 2 biscuits • half a slice of cake • 1 doughnut • 1 Danish pastry • 1 small bar of chocolate • 1 small tube or bag of sweets.

Too salty

Salt (sodium chloride) is essential for a variety of body functions, but we tend to eat too much through consumption of salty processed foods, 'fast' foods and ready-prepared foods, and by adding salt in cooking and at the table. The end result can be rising blood pressure as we get older, which puts us at higher risk of heart disease and stroke. Eating more vegetables and fruit increases potassium intake, which can help to counteract the damaging effects of salt.

Alcohol in a healthy diet

In recent research, moderate drinking of alcohol has been linked with a reduced risk of heart disease and stroke among men and women over 45. However, because of other risks associated with alcohol, particularly in excessive quantities, no doctor would recommend taking up drinking if you are teetotal. The healthiest pattern of drinking is to enjoy small amounts of alcohol with food, to have alcohol-free days and always to avoid getting drunk. A well-balanced diet is vital because nutrients from food (vitamins and minerals) are needed to detoxify the alcohol.

Water – the best choice

Drinking plenty of non-alcoholic liquid each day is an often overlooked part of a well-balanced diet. A minimum of 8 glasses (which is about 2 litres/3½ pints) is the ideal. If possible, these should not all be tea or coffee, as these are stimulants and diuretics, which cause the body to lose liquids, taking with them water-soluble vitamins. Water is the best choice. Other good choices are fruit or herb teas or tisanes, fruit juices – diluted with water, if preferred – or semi-skimmed milk (full-fat milk for very young children). Fizzy sugary or acidic drinks such as cola are more likely to damage tooth enamel than other drinks.

As a guide to the vitamin and mineral content of foods and recipes in the book, we have used the following terms and symbols, based on the percentage of the daily RNI provided by one serving for the average adult man or woman aged 19–49 years (see also pages 156–158):

✓✓✓	or excellent	at least 50% (half)
✓✓	or good	25–50% (one-quarter to one-half)
✓	or useful	10–25% (one-tenth to one-quarter)

Note that recipes contribute other nutrients, but the analyses only include those that provide at least 10% RNI per portion. Vitamins and minerals where deficiencies are rare are not included.

Ⓥ denotes that a recipe is suitable for vegetarians.

Versatile Rice, Beans and Grains

Making a great contribution to the modern diet

Here are the new stars of good cooking – cereal grains and pulses. Today, they are found on all the most fashionable restaurant menus and in recipe books galore. It's no wonder, with such a wide array of colourful varieties to choose from, and the amazing range of delicious dishes that can be created with them. The fact that they are also among the most nutritious foods you can eat is a fantastic bonus. So if you haven't cooked much with rice, grains and pulses in the past, now is the time to join the growing army of 'bean cuisine' fans.

Healthy rice, beans and grains

Rice, beans and grains are probably the cheapest of all the food groups, so everyone can benefit from the high levels of nutrients they offer – vital starchy carbohydrates, protein, minerals, vitamins and dietary fibre. They are also low in the 'not so good' items, such as saturated fat and sodium.

Why eat rice, beans and grains?

Most of the calories in grains and pulses are in the form of starchy carbohydrate, which should contribute at least 50% of the calories in our daily diet. In addition, wholegrains (those that are unrefined) and all pulses are high in natural fibre. Beans also contain protein, which makes them especially useful for vegetarians. Indeed, for thousands of years they have been a main source of protein in many parts of the world. Grains and pulses also provide a a variety of phytochemicals – compounds that are believed to have many health benefits.

Divine rice

Originating in China and India, rice has been a staple of the diet there for thousands of years, as well as in other parts of Asia, Africa and South America. Today, it is estimated that more rice is eaten than any other cereal crop. Indeed, rice is revered as divine in many communities, and when it was first introduced into ancient Greece it was more highly prized than Beluga caviar is today!

Like other cereals, rice is low in fat. It contains some protein although less than other cereals. Because it contains no gluten, it is an ideal alternative to grains such as wheat, barley and oats for people with coeliac disease (gluten intolerance).

- Brown rice is often called wholegrain rice, a term that isn't strictly true as the outer, inedible husk is removed. But all the rest of the grain remains intact, including the outer bran layers and the germ in the centre. Brown rice is a good source of most B vitamins, except B_{12}. It also contains a good range of minerals, such as magnesium and copper.
- White (polished) rice has had the husk and germ removed. It keeps longer than brown rice because when the husk and germ are removed, rice becomes harder, with less tendency to spoil. Polishing the grain to achieve white rice removes most of the fibre and B vitamins and a high proportion of the minerals.

Bran and minerals

It has been thought that the bran in brown rice and wholegrains might hinder the body's uptake of minerals such as iron and calcium. This is because bran contains phytic acid, which binds with the minerals, rendering them indigestible. However, studies show that bran eaten as part of a wholegrain is less likely to have this effect than bran extracted from a grain and used separately – wheat bran sprinkled onto cereals, for example. There is also some evidence to show that eating foods rich in essential fatty acids (e.g. oily fish and nuts) at the same time may counteract the possible adverse effect of the bran and aid absorption of the minerals. Until we know more, the sensible solution is to enjoy brown rice and wholegrains, and to eat plenty of calcium and iron-rich foods at other times. And to remember that wholegrains have positive effects on health in all other respects.

Pulses for cheap protein

The generic (family) name for all dried beans, lentils and dried peas is pulses. Although their individual nutrient content varies, pulses are, as a family, an important source of non-animal protein as well as starchy carbohydrate and fibre. Pulses are highly adaptable, able to be used as the protein, starchy carbohydrate or vegetable element in a meal.

Most pulses are rich in folate and other B vitamins, and some are good sources of vitamin E, as well as a wide range of minerals, including magnesium and iron. The nutritional content of pulses increases dramatically when they are sprouted – there is 60% more vitamin C and almost 30% more B vitamins in the sprout than in the original bean.

▲ Rice can be used in lots of imaginative and nutritious ways, such as in these tasty Rice pancakes with an onion and spinach topping (see Some more ideas, page 53)

▲ Try a grain dish such as Dilled barley and smoked salmon salad for a delicious lunch or supper (see Some more ideas, page 95)

▼ Make a hearty Roast vegetable and bean stew (see page 108), using butternut squash, and serve with jacket baked potatoes

Grains make good eating

In many regions of the world, grains make up a large part of every meal, and cereal crops such as wheat, barley and oats are the most important plant food available. In the West, wheat is the most-grown cereal crop, used to make bread, pasta and many other popular foods.

Wholegrains (those that still retain all of their layers, including the bran and germ) contain considerably more dietary fibre than grains that have been highly milled (such as white flour). As such, wholegrains have been linked with lowered risk of bowel cancer and diverticular disease, and can help to prevent constipation. Wholegrains also contain several of the B-group vitamins, including folate, which may help to protect against heart disease. When grains are refined they lose a large percentage of their vitamins and minerals.

All grains contribute valuable starchy carbohydrate as well as some protein.

Wild about rice

All rice is 'good for you' and can be eaten as frequently as you like, within a **varied healthy diet**. The flavour and texture of rice are only improved by cooking it with other **ingredients** or serving it with a sauce. It makes a tasty alternative to potatoes or pasta, **and there are** lots of different rices to choose from.

Different types of rice

Rice is classified by the size of its grain – long, medium and short – and varieties range in texture from fluffy to creamy to sticky. Colour varies from brown to white to red. The shape, size, texture and other characteristics of the different varieties affect the way the rice is used in recipes – what types of dish it is suitable for and the way it is cooked. Each country favours particular varieties for its cuisine.

Long-grain rices

Long-grain rice, as the name suggests, has grains that are long and slim. When cooked, the grains tend to remain separate, and the finished result is usually fairly dry and firm.

Basmati rice With very long, slim grains, basmati is often called the 'king' of rices, as it has excellent cooking qualities and a full flavour. It is grown only in northern India and Pakistan, and no other rice can be labelled as basmati. It also comes in a wholegrain form, which tends to be lighter and quicker to cook than other brown rices. The extra nutritional advantage of basmati rice is that it scores low on the Glycaemic Index – its carbohydrate content is absorbed less quickly into the bloodstream than other types of rice, and thus it helps to keep blood sugar levels stable. Basmati rice should be rinsed before cooking to get rid of the starchy powder left over from milling.

Long-grain rice This is usually the patna or Carolina varieties of rice (sometimes it will be labelled as such). Most is in a polished white form, although brown long-grain rice is also available. Patna rice comes from Asia; Carolina rice, which is slightly chunkier in appearance, is from North America.

Parboiled rice Sometimes called 'converted' rice or 'processed' rice, this is wholegrain rice that is soaked, steamed and dried before milling and polishing. The process forces the vitamins and minerals into the centre of the grain so that more are retained than in ordinary white rice. The colour of this rice is more golden than other white rice and it takes a little longer to cook. Even with over-cooking, the grains will remain separate.

Quick-cook rice Also called easy-cook rice, this shouldn't be confused with parboiled rice. Quick-cook rice is part-cooked after milling and then dried, so that when you cook it, it takes about half the time of ordinary long-grain rice. Quick-cook rice has lost most of its nutrients, especially the water-soluble B vitamins, because of this 'double-cook' process.

Red rice A wholegrain rice with a red outer skin, this has a nutty flavour and slightly chewy texture. The best quality red rice comes from the Camargue region of France; other red rices, produced in North America, are also available.

Thai fragrant rice Also known as jasmine rice, this is grown in eastern Asia. It has a slight perfume and when cooked is slightly more sticky than other long-grain rices. It marries well with other Asian foods and is the rice to use in Thai cookery.

New strains of long-grain rice

New types of rice are being produced in North America, Australia and other parts of the world. Texmati is the USA's version of basmati, created to satisfy the huge world demand for this type of rice – true basmati can only be produced in relatively small amounts in India and Pakistan. Two other new American long-grain rices are wahani, suitable for Asian cooking, and wild pecan rice, which has a mild nutty flavour. Doongara is a new Australian rice, similar to basmati.

basmati rice

long-grain rice

red rice

parboiled rice

Thai fragrant rice

quick-cook rice

13

Chinese black rice

glutinous rice

Japanese sushi rice

Wild rice

Wild rice is not, in fact, a member of the rice family but a type of grass. It is native to the Minnesota Lakes area of the USA and was first harvested by the North American Indians. Most of the wild rice now sold is grown commercially in artificial ponds. Dark brown in colour, with very long, thin, pointed grains, it has a distinctive, strong flavour. Its protein content is higher than other rices and it contains twice as much folate as ordinary brown rice. It can be used on its own, when its cooking time is quite long, but it is more usually mixed with white or brown long-grain rice. When sold mixed with white rice, the outer skin has been broken to shorten the cooking time.

Short and medium-grain rices

These rices contain a starchy substance called amylopectin, which causes stickiness (long-grain rice has much less of this starch). After cooking, the individual grains cling together, which is why these rices are used in dishes where a creamy or sticky texture is wanted, such as risottos, puddings and sushi.

Chinese black rice An unrefined rice, this has a brownish-black skin and flattish, wide grains. It is usually soaked and then steamed. In Asia it is also used to make a dessert with coconut milk and palm sugar.

Glutinous rice Sometimes referred to as 'Chinese rice' or 'sticky rice', this is widely used in South-east Asia for both sweet and savoury dishes. Its grains are almost round and chalky-white. Ironically, the name is misleading as, like all other rices, it contains no gluten. The normal cooking method is to soak and then steam it, after which the grains stick together as if with glue. This means it can be eaten in small balls picked up with the fingers or chopsticks.

Japanese sushi rice A short-grain rice, this is usually soaked and then cooked by the absorption method. Once cooled, it is

pudding rice

sweet brown rice

paella rice

risotto rice

Rice in other forms

Being gluten-free, rice products are suitable for people with a wheat or gluten intolerance.

Ground rice is white rice coarsely milled to the consistency of semolina. It can be used in puddings and baby food.

Rice cakes are discs of rice that have been baked. They are low in fat and calories, and can be a tasty substitute for bread, wheat crackers or crispbreads.

Rice flakes are produced by parboiling and then flattening rice between rollers before drying. They are quick to cook and can be used in puddings, or added to stews as a thickener.

Rice flour is a fine-milled flour (with a finer texture than ground rice), which can either be wholegrain or white. It is useful for baking and bread-making.

Rice noodles are fine, translucent noodles made from rice flour, used in South-east Asian cooking. They come in several shapes and sizes, and are quick to cook.

Rice vinegar is made from fermented rice.

Rice wine, also called sake (or saki) is, in fact, a flat beer made from fermented steamed rice and water. It is pale in colour, with a sweet taste and a slightly bitter aftertaste. Mirin is a golden wine made from glutinous rice.

flavoured with sweetened rice vinegar and rolled up in nori seaweed with other ingredients such as raw fish or vegetables to make sushi. The stickiness of the rice holds the sushi rolls together.

Paella rice From the Spanish region of Valencia, this is used in the traditional dish of Spain, paella. It is a plump, short-grain rice similar to risotto rice, but with a less creamy texture.

Pudding rice This short-grain rice is very similar to risotto rice, but with sweeter-tasting grains. It needs long, slow cooking and produces a silky, creamy texture, which is why it is used to make rice puddings. It should not be used for savoury dishes, even risottos, as the taste will be disappointing.

Risotto rice The famous medium-grain rice of Italy, this has plump, white, oval grains. When cooked with liquid stirred in slowly, the grains retain their individual shape yet become creamy. Arborio is the best-known of the risotto rices, but of even better quality are Carnaroli and Vialone Nano.

Sweet brown rice Called *mochi* in Japan, this is a sweet-flavoured, very glutinous rice with a high starch content. It is used to make rice cakes and sweet confections.

Clockwise from back left: rice wine, mirin, rice vinegar, rice noodles, ground rice, rice flour, rice cakes

versatile rice, beans and grains

15

Basic rice cookery

Rice can be cooked in all sorts of different ways – boiled, steamed, stir-fried, simmered or baked – to make a wonderful variety of dishes. Some methods minimise the loss of valuable water-soluble B vitamins, by ensuring that none of the nutrients are discarded with the cooking water. But however you cook it, rice is good for you.

Cooking long-grain rice

Long-grain rice is usually cooked by boiling, which can either be open boiling or the absorption method. The latter produces very tasty rice with a good texture, and it retains a high proportion of the nutrients because all the water used is absorbed into the rice. Long-grain rice can also be steamed and microwaved.

The absorption method

To cook one of the white long-grain rices by this method, first weigh out the quantity specified in a recipe. Then, if no liquid quantity is specified, tip the rice into a measuring jug – you need about twice the volume of water to rice.

Put the rice and water in a heavy-based saucepan that has a tight-fitting lid and bring to the boil. When the water is boiling, turn the heat down to low so the water is very gently simmering. Give the pan's contents a good stir with a fork, and put the lid on. Leave to cook, covered, for 10–15 minutes (or according to the packet instructions).

To test if the rice is ready, lift out a few grains on a fork. If the rice still seems too firm but all the water has been absorbed, add a little more boiling water and simmer for a few more minutes. When the rice is tender, remove the pan from the heat and set aside to rest for a few minutes. This will allow the rice to absorb any last traces of water. (The rice will retain its heat if you keep the lid on, and you can slip a clean teatowel between the pan and the lid to help dry out the rice.) Finally, fluff up the rice lightly with a fork to separate the grains, and serve.

Wholegrain long-grain rices (brown rice, wild rice and red rice) can also be cooked by the absorption method, but need more water – 2½ times the volume of water to rice – and longer cooking. Brown basmati rice takes about 25 minutes; other long-grain brown rices, wild rice and red rice need 30–40 minutes cooking.

Boiling

Long-grain rice can simply be cooked in a large volume of fast-boiling water, in which case it will take 10–15 minutes for white rice or 30–35 minutes for wholegrain. When tender, it should be drained in a sieve. This method can result in soft, mushy, tasteless rice if you overcook it.

Steaming

The aborption method is, in fact, a type of steaming, but rice can also be cooked in a steamer over boiling water. In China, a traditional bamboo steamer is used lined with muslin. The rice is soaked for up to 1 hour, then drained, put into the muslin-lined steamer and steamed for 20 minutes or until tender. This method is used for both long-grain rices and glutinous rice.

Microwaving

Long-grain rice can be cooked very successfully in the microwave, using the absorption method. Measure 1 part rice to 2 parts water and cook in a microwavable basin, with a lid lightly resting on the top, for 12 minutes. Leave to stand for 5 minutes, still covered, then stir before serving.

Using an electric rice cooker

If you eat a lot of rice, you might want to invest in an electric rice cooker. Rice cooked in a rice cooker has a slightly different texture from that cooked in a pan, but the finished result is always acceptable if the manufacturer's instructions are followed.

cooking long-grain rice by the absorption method

Cooking other rices

Short-grain and medium-grain rices tend to be cooked by longer, slower techniques than those used for long-grain rice. Sometimes a combination of methods is used.

- **Glutinous rice and sushi rice** These sticky rices are usually soaked for 30 minutes before steaming or cooking by the absorption method.
- **Paella and risotto rices** These are an integral part of a recipe, not cooked separately. For a risotto, the normal method is to 'toast' the uncooked rice in hot oil, then to gradually add hot liquid such as stock or water. Each addition of liquid should be almost all absorbed before the next is added, and the rice is stirred almost constantly. At the end of cooking, the rice will be creamy and tender but with a firm centre. Paella rice is cooked by a similar method, but the liquid may be added all at once and it is not usually stirred during cooking.

cooking risotto rice

- **Pudding rice** White pudding rice needs long, slow cooking in liquid (usually milk) to produce a traditional rice pudding. Black rice is cooked in coconut milk for a Chinese version.

Storing and reheating cooked rice

Cooked rice can be stored in a covered container in the fridge for a day or so. It should always be kept cool, as otherwise it could develop toxins that can cause food poisoning. For longer keeping, rice freezes well.

Rice can be reheated in a steamer, or in the microwave, loosely covered, for 1–2 minutes or until piping hot. Another way to reheat cooked rice is by using it in a stir-fry.

steaming long-grain rice

Getting to know pulses

When planning healthy meals, it's well worth making use of the family of pulses – dried beans, lentils and peas. Being low in fat, high in dietary fibre and wonderfully nutritious, they have a lot to offer. Also, many of the vitamins and minerals they provide are not always so easy to come by in vegetarian and fast-food diets.

Why are pulses important?

Almost all of the pulses contain a near-perfect balance of starchy carbohydrate and protein – roughly 50% of their calorie content comes from carbohydrate, which is almost all starchy, or complex, rather than simple carbohydrate or sugars, and 20–30% from protein.

• Pulses are an important source of protein for people trying to cut down their animal and dairy intake, and for vegetarians and vegans. The protein provided by most pulses does not contain all 8 of the essential amino acids – the building blocks of protein (soya beans are the one exception) – but the nutritional value of pulse protein is easily enhanced by eating them with pasta, rice or other grains, or with small quantities of lean meat, which contain the 'missing' amino acids.

• Most pulses are excellent sources of both soluble and insoluble fibre. Soluble fibre has been shown to lower blood cholesterol as part of an overall diet low in fat. Insoluble fibre is important for digestive health and may help to prevent colon cancer and diverticular disease.

• Pulses in general are very low in fat and only a small percentage of the fat is saturated; much of the remainder is in the form of the essential fatty acids, omega-3 and omega-6, which have many health benefits.

• Many pulses are good sources of B vitamins, including folate, and vitamin E. They are also good sources of iron, zinc and magnesium, all of which may be in short supply in a modern, fast-food diet, as well as in vegetarian and vegan diets where meat – normally a main source of supply – is excluded. To aid absorption of these minerals, try to eat pulses with a vitamin C-rich food, such as fresh vegetables, potatoes or fruit. Many types of beans contain some calcium too.

An ABC of beans

There are hundreds of different varieties of dried beans throughout the world. Here is a selection of those that you are most likely to come across (numbers refer to the picture on the opposite page).

1 Aduki bean This is a very small, roundish, dark red bean with a slightly sweet taste. Popular in Japan and the Far East, it is used in a variety of dishes, both savoury and sweet. Aduki beans are higher in protein than many other pulses.

2 Black bean (Chinese) A variety of soya bean, this is a medium-small, round, shiny black bean. It is normally fermented and salted, which gives it a rich savoury flavour. In Chinese cookery, fermented black beans are often mashed with a little sugar and water and added to dishes as a paste.

3 Black kidney bean Similar in shape and size to the red kidney bean, this has a black skin and a white flesh; it turns brown on cooking. Popular in Central and South America, black kidney beans are used to make the Brazilian national dish, feijoada.

4 Black-eyed bean Popular in Caribbean cookery as well as in India and the Mediterranean, this is a pale, oval bean with a black 'eye'. It has a creamy texture with a slightly sweet flavour, and is good used in soups and casseroles.

5 Broad bean Also called fava or faba bean, this is the dried form of our garden broad bean. Large, flat and pale brown, with an earthy flavour, it is most often added to casseroles.

6 Borlotti bean This attractive, medium-sized bean, pale pink speckled with brown, comes from Italy. Being soft-textured it makes a creamy purée and is delicious in soups and salads.

7 Cannellini bean A variety of haricot bean grown widely in Italy, the cannellini is medium-large, cream-coloured and mild but pleasant in taste. Cannellini beans are good in soups, salads and casseroles, and go well in fish dishes, particularly those made with tuna.

versatile rice, beans and grains

8 Butter bean Originating from South America, this is a very large, flattish bean with an attractive deep cream colour. There is a hint of potato in the flavour. Butter beans purée well and can be used as a side dish or dip; they also make good soup. Lima beans are a close relation but slightly smaller.

9 Ful medames (Egyptian brown bean) Small, round and mid-brown, with a full flavour, this is a variety of broad bean. It is native to Egypt where, combined with eggs, garlic and spices, it is made into the national dish of the same name. Ful medames are widely used in the Eastern Mediterranean.

10 Flageolet Popular in France and Italy, this is a medium-sized, pale green bean with a delicate yet distinctive flavour. It keeps its attractive colour when cooked, and is ideal in salads.

11 Pinto bean Looking like a borlotti bean but a little smaller, the pinto bean comes from Central and South America. With its creamy texture, it is good in soups.

12 Haricot bean This is the bean used for 'baked beans', so popular throughout the Western world – no wonder it is one of the most widely grown of all beans. Medium-sized and pale cream in colour, it is also the classic bean to use in a French cassoulet. Haricot beans contain more soluble fibre than any other pulse.

13 Soya bean Much harder than other beans, the soya bean needs very long soaking and cooking. It is also quite bland, so needs to be cooked with strongly flavoured ingredients, such as onion, tomato, spices or herbs. One of the world's biggest crops, soya beans are converted into many other kinds of food.

14 Red kidney bean This red-skinned bean, with meaty white flesh, keeps its colour on cooking and absorbs other flavours well. Its robust taste and texture means it works well in hot, spicy dishes, such as chilli con carne.

A word about soya beans

The soya is the only bean that contains all 8 amino acids. Soya beans are unique in other ways too. For example, the iron they provide is better absorbed by the body than the iron in other pulses. Soya beans are also a good source of calcium – an important point for vegans who don't eat dairy products. They contain more omega-3 and omega-6 fatty acids than other pulses, and offer more soluble fibre than most.

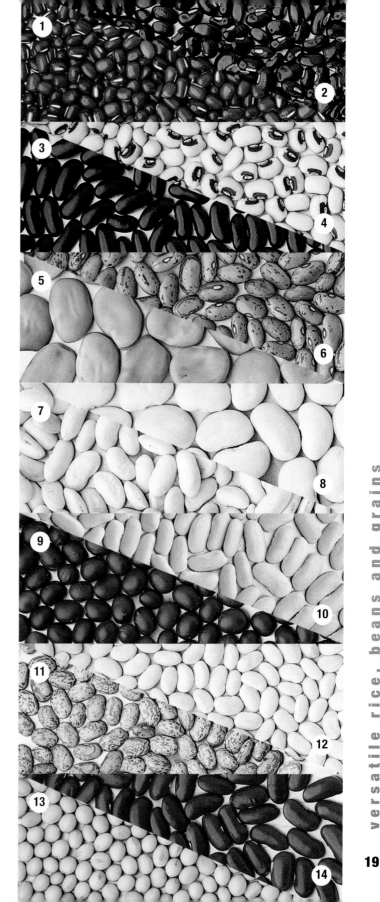

An ABC of lentils and peas

These seeds of leguminous plants make up the rest of the family of pulses.

Chana dal A small, brown relation of the chickpea, this is usually sold split – it looks similar to yellow split peas. Chana dal have a slightly sweet flavour and are widely used in Indian and Middle Eastern cookery for dal or as part of a pilau. They are usually only available from Indian grocers. In India, it is chana dal that is used to make chickpea flour, rather than the larger chickpea from the Mediterranean region.

Chickpea Despite the name, this is not really a pea but a seed. Medium-sized, round and beige, it is widely used in North Africa and the Eastern Mediterranean as well as in India. Chickpeas are the main ingredient of hummus and of falafel. They are richer in vitamin E than most other pulses.

Gunga pea (pigeon pea) Round, smooth, medium-sized and usually brown, this pea comes from Africa. It is much used in Indian cookery for dal.

Lentil Grown mainly around the eastern Mediterranean and in India, the lentil is one of the world's oldest crops. Brown or green 'continental' lentils are very tasty, and retain their shape well after cooking, so are ideal in salads or as a vegetable accompaniment. They also purée well and add richness and texture to soups and casseroles. Grey-green Puy lentils are a small variety grown only in the Puy region of France. They have an excellent flavour. Red and yellow lentils are normally available split in half. They cook very quickly and can be easily puréed. All brown and green lentils are good sources of vitamin B_6, folate and iron; split lentils are less nutritious because the outer layer of the lentil has been removed.

Mung bean Native to Asia, this small, cylindrical-shaped green seed is most often used for sprouting, and is the familiar 'bean sprout'. It can also be used as a vegetable in a variety of dishes, and marries very well with rice and Indian spices.

Split pea Usually green or yellow in colour, this is a dried pea that has had its outer skin removed and has then been split in half. Split peas can be cooked to serve as a side vegetable, used in casseroles and soups, or puréed. They have less fibre, vitamins and minerals than most other pulses, but are a useful source of protein.

Urd (gram) This very small pea looks a little like a darker version of a mung bean. Available whole or split, it can be used like mung beans, or puréed.

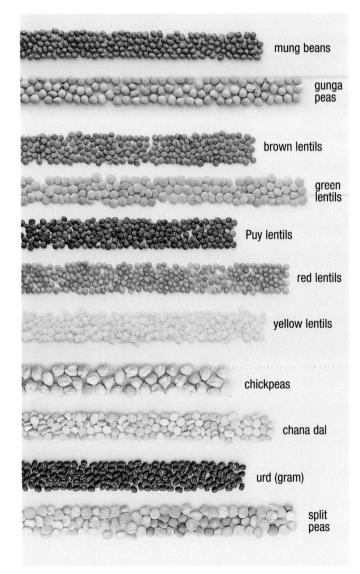

mung beans

gunga peas

brown lentils

green lentils

Puy lentils

red lentils

yellow lentils

chickpeas

chana dal

urd (gram)

split peas

versatile rice, beans and grains

Bean products

The humble bean – particularly the soya bean – can be transformed into a wide variety of other foods. Here are a few of them.

Black and yellow bean sauces are made from crushed or puréed, fermented black or cream-coloured soya beans. They are sold in cans, jars or sachets, usually with additions such as vinegar, oil, sugar or garlic.

Cellophone noodles, also called transparent or bean thread noodles, are made from the starch of the mung bean. Fine and white, they are soaked in water or stock before use, which makes them slippery and translucent. They are used in soups and stir-fries. In Chinese cooking they are also often deep-fried in hot oil.

Chickpea flour (besan, gram flour) is made by grinding dried chickpeas (or, in India, chana dal) until fine. It is used in Indian cookery for thickening and to make batters.

Miso is a thick paste made from fermented soya beans. It is useful for flavouring casseroles and stews, but is quite salty.

Soya milk is a useful alternative to cow's milk for vegans and people allergic to dairy products. It is high in protein, with a similar fat content to semi-skimmed milk, and is often fortified with calcium.

Soy sauce is a thin, dark brown sauce made from soya beans fermented with barley or wheat. Naturally fermented soy sauce, called shoyu or tamari, is considered to be superior to the less expensive, commercial soy sauces which usually contain sugar and other additives.

Tofu is a pale cream, high-protein food manufactured from soya beans. Firm tofu, sold in blocks (often vacuum-packed or in water), has a texture similar to that of feta cheese. It can be sliced and used in stir-fries, casseroles and many other dishes as a substitute for meat; although very bland, it soaks up other flavours well. Silken tofu has a creamier texture and is useful for making non-dairy, low-fat dips and a mayonnaise-like salad dressing.

TVP (textured vegetable protein) is soya that has been manufactured to look like mince or small chunks of meat, and can be used in recipes in the same way that you would use minced beef or lamb. TVP is usually sold dry, in bags, although it also comes in cans and frozen.

From left to right: bean sauce, TVP mince, soy sauce, soya milk, miso, cellophane noodles, TVP chunks, tofu, chickpea flour

Basic pulse cookery

Drying is a simple way of preserving pulses so that they can be stored for months, keeping most of their protein content intact and retaining their flavour. It does mean, though, that most dried pulses need to be soaked before cooking. Canned pulses are already cooked and need only to be drained and rinsed.

A soak to rehydrate

Soaking pulses ensures that they will cook evenly and relatively quickly. It may also help to get rid of some of the substances called oligosaccharides that cause flatulence, although most of these are lost when the pulses are cooked. How long a dried pulse needs to be soaked depends on the variety as well as on how long it has been stored.

Lentils and split peas need no soaking at all, whereas most dried beans, chickpeas and other whole peas should be soaked for at least 8 hours. Soya beans are notorious for needing longer-than-average soaking and are best left overnight. In hot weather, it's a good idea to soak pulses in the refrigerator.

Recently-dried pulses – such as the dried flageolets you see in France in the autumn, labelled 'new season' – tend not to need such a long soak, whereas pulses that have been stored a long time, and are thus even more dried out, may need longer soaking than is normally recommended.

A good rule-of-thumb for telling when a pulse has been soaked long enough is that there will be no wrinkling remaining on the skin. The pulse will look plump and have increased in size, sometimes up to 3 times the original size.

Pulses can be soaked longer than 8–12 hours, although if they are left for more than 1–2 days, they will begin to sprout and ferment. (If you want to sprout them, you need to rinse them and refresh the water regularly – see the box opposite for instructions.)

After soaking, drain and rinse the pulses. Discard the soaking water and use fresh water for cooking.

Fast boiling

There are toxic proteins (lectins or haemoglutigens) contained in the outer layers of most pulses, which cannot be digested in the stomach, and which may cause symptoms of severe food poisoning such as diarrhoea and vomiting. This is of special concern for people with poor digestion, the elderly and those convalescing from illness. Red kidney beans and soya beans are particularly high in these toxins.

A short period of rapid boiling will effectively destroy the toxins, so a 10–15 minute fast boil at the start of cooking has always been recommended for red kidney beans and soya beans. However, current advice is that all pulses – with the exception of chickpeas, gunga peas, lentils and split peas – should be given a fast boil before cooking begins.

Cooking

Once pulses have been given their fast boil, reduce the heat so the liquid is just simmering. Skim the froth from the surface, then partly cover the pan and leave to cook gently until the pulses are tender, topping up with more boiling water as necessary. The length of the simmering time depends on the variety of pulse and how dry it is. For example, dried haricot beans can take 50 minutes to 1½ hours, and chickpeas from 1 to 3 hours. Soya beans take the longest time to cook – 2½ to 4 hours. Recipes in the book give tested cooking times, but you may prefer to follow the instructions on the packet. Do not salt the cooking water, because this may toughen the pulses and prolong the cooking time – instead, add salt and other seasonings at the end of cooking. It is also not advisable to add bicarbonate of soda to the cooking water, as this can adversely affect both flavour and nutritional value.

Pulses are sometimes cooked in water before being added to a casserole that will be cooked further (such as when making baked beans or chilli con carne). If the sauce mixture contains an acidic ingredient such as tomatoes, the pulses will not become any softer. So they must be thoroughly cooked and tender before they are added to the casserole.

Canned pulses, which are already cooked, can be used cold or reheated gently to serve hot.

Sprouting pulses

Bean and other pulse sprouts make a crisp and nutritious addition to salads and stir-fries, providing useful amounts of B vitamins, especially folate, and vitamin C. The bean sprouts you are most likely to find in the shops are from mung and aduki beans, but many other pulses can be sprouted successfully. Whole green and brown lentils and chickpeas are particularly good.

You can buy special layered sprouting containers, which are useful if you want to sprout different varieties at the same time. Here's how to do it the simple way.

- Rinse the pulses, then place in a large jar (a kilner-type jar is ideal). Fill the jar with water, then cover with a piece of muslin secured with an elastic band. Leave to soak in a warm place overnight.

- The next day, pour off the water through the muslin, then refill the jar with water through the muslin. Shake gently, then drain off the water and leave the jar on its side (**top right**), away from direct sunlight.

- Twice a day, rinse the pulses well with water and drain. After a few days they will begin to sprout (**middle right**).

- When the shoots are 1–2 cm (½–¾ in) long, place the jar in a sunny but not too hot place. Leave for a few more days, still rinsing regularly, until they have grown to the desired size (**bottom right**).

- Rinse well and remove any ungerminated beans before using. The sprouts can be kept in a plastic bag in the fridge for 1–2 days.

- Eat the sprouts as fresh as possible and before their seed leaves form.

Going for grains

Grains – the large family of cultivated botanical grasses – have been grown for food since the Stone Age. The earliest cereal-growing communities developed in the fertile lands of what are now Iraq, Turkey and Jordan. Then, grains were the major source of starchy carbohydrate in the diet. Today, they are still the 'staff of life'.

An ABC of grains

Every great civilisation has been founded on agriculture – the growing of wheat, barley, rye, rice, oats and corn – with the staple grain varying according to the geographic location and growing conditions. Wheat and rye were most important in the West, and rice and millet were the staples of the East, with maize being the primary crop of Africa and central and south America. Nowadays, these divisions are much less noticeable, with different grains being grown all over the world, for export to almost anywhere. The wide and exciting range of grains can be used to bring variety, flavour and good nutrition to your table.

Those grains that are gluten-free – buckwheat, maize, millet and quinoa – are ideal for people who are gluten-intolerant.

Barley

In early times, barley was often used to make bread. Now that is rarely so, but barley is regaining popularity as a grain that is versatile and rich in nutrients, in particular vitamin B_6, niacin, potassium and iron. Like other grains, when barley is refined, it loses much of its vitamin and mineral content – for example, the vitamin B_1 content is depleted by 60% in its pearl barley form.

Barley flakes are made from whole grains of barley, which are processed into flakes and dried. They are suitable for use in muesli (and make a good alternative for people with a wheat allergy). They can also be cooked as a porridge.

Barley meal is produced by grinding barley grains into a meal or flour, which can be used in breads and bakes or stirred into soups and casseroles to thicken them.

barley • barley meal • pot barley • barley flakes • pearl barley • unroasted buckwheat • kasha (roasted buckwheat)

Pearl barley is made by milling the whole barley grain to remove the outer layers, leaving the pale interior. Pearl barley is a good source of low-fat, easily digested complex (starchy) carbohydrate and is most often used in soups and casseroles, although it also works well in salads. The starch in the grains is easily released and acts as a thickener.

Pot barley is the whole grain of barley, rich in starchy carbohydrate, and containing much more dietary fibre, particularly soluble fibre, than any other cereal. Pot barley can be cooked in a similar way to rice as a side dish or to use in salads and pilafs. It has a nutty flavour, similar to brown rice.

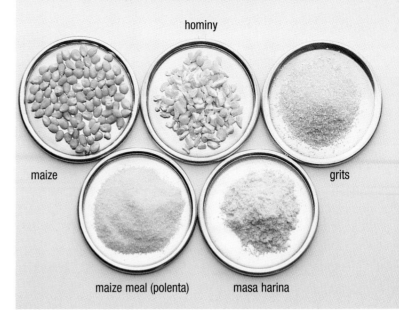

hominy

maize

grits

maize meal (polenta)

masa harina

Buckwheat

This isn't really a cereal grain, but the seed of a plant that is a member of the rhubarb family. However, the seeds are grain-like, and it is cooked like a grain. Buckwheat is higher in protein than many other grains, and also contains excellent amounts of iron, calcium, vitamin E and B vitamins.

Kasha is the name frequently given to whole buckwheat grains (often cracked) that have been toasted or roasted. It is also the name of a porridge-like dish popular in Asia and Eastern Europe. Kasha makes an excellent and tasty substitute for rice and is good in spicy risotto-like dishes because the grains tend to break down when cooked.

Unroasted buckwheat grains are crushed and hulled grains, pale green-grey in colour, which can be cooked like rice. They are good with any savoury dish or for stuffing vegetables. You can toast or roast (both terms are used) your own buckwheat for an even better flavour and texture – spread the grains on a baking tray and cook in a preheated 180°C (350°F, gas mark 4) oven until they turn golden brown.

Maize

Maize is one of the world's most versatile crops. It can be harvested before the grains have matured for sweetcorn cobs, to be eaten as a vegetable. Left to mature, the maize grains can be harvested to be milled or left whole for a variety of uses (depending upon the type of maize), for example as breakfast cornflakes and popcorn. Others are ground into fine or coarse meals and flours. Maize is a good source of iron, but lower in the other nutrients typical of most grains. Yellow maize contains antioxidant carotenes, but white forms don't.

Hominy is dried white or yellow corn kernels, whole or broken into particles, from which the husk and germ have been removed. Hominy is sold canned, ready-to eat or dried; if dried, it needs to be softened by boiling in water or milk. It can be fried, baked or added to a casserole. Grits are ground hominy and may be fine, medium or coarse. They are generally simmered in water or milk until very thick, to make a breakfast dish or an accompaniment to meat dishes. Because hominy and hominy grits have had the germ and outer husk removed, their nutrient content is reduced. In the USA, where hominy and grits are popular, they are usually enriched with B vitamins and iron.

Maize meal (cornmeal, polenta) is ground corn, which comes in various textures from a powder to a coarse meal. It contains about 95% of the whole grain and is a good source of iron. Dishes made from maize meal, such as porridge, pancakes and bread, are an easily digested form of starchy carbohydrate. One of the most popular ways of using cornmeal is in the traditional Northern Italian dish polenta, when the meal is cooked with water or stock until it thickens; it can then either

whole oats

oat flakes

coarse oatmeal

fine oatmeal

millet

millet flakes

be eaten soft, like a purée, or set. Special polenta cornmeal can be bought, which is bright yellow with a granular texture similar to semolina.

Masa harina, or tamale flour, is the flour used to make corn tortillas. Dried corn kernels are soaked and then cooked in limewater (water mixed with calcium oxide), before they are ground to a meal and dried.

Millet

This very small, golden cereal grain, native to Asia and Africa, has a delicate, slightly nutty flavour. It contains useful amounts of many of the B vitamins, as well as more iron than other cereals and higher levels of protein than some.

Millet, in its wholegrain form, can be cooked in a similar way to other wholegrains – it absorbs up to 4 times its own weight in water. It can be used to stuff vegetables, as part of a burger mix.

Millet flakes can be added to casseroles, soups and stews. Sorghum is a larger relative of millet and can be used in similar ways.

Oats

Oats are native to Eastern Europe but are probably best known as the main ingredient in porridge. Oats contain approximately twice as much fat as most other cereals, and they tend to go rancid quickly unless they have been through a steaming process before packaging, so they are best stored in a cool, dark place (preferably the fridge).

Oats can help to reduce blood cholesterol levels when eaten regularly, particularly if consumed with a low-fat diet, and thus may help to prevent coronary heart disease. They can also help to keep blood sugar levels stable, as they score low on the Glycaemic Index.

Oat flakes/rolled oats are whole oat grains that have simply been husked, then flattened or rolled, and thus contain virtually all of the vitamins and minerals in the whole grain.

'Steelcut' oats may retain more of the essential fats in the oat because this process does not use heat, which destroys these fats. Oats can be cooked with water and/or milk to make porridge, eaten raw, or used in baking.

Oatmeal, which is milled oat grains, comes in varying degrees of coarseness. The fine variety can be used in biscuits, bread and oatcakes, while coarser varieties can be used to make porridge. Instant oatmeal is a quick breakast cereal, but contains fewer nutrients than oat flakes/rolled oats.

Whole oats are whole oat grains (also known as kernels or groats). They can be bought in healthfood shops and used like brown rice or pot barley.

Quinoa

Quinoa (pronounced 'keen-wah') is a small, yellowy-brown, South American grain that is becoming more widely available elsewhere. It should be rinsed well before cooking, to remove the slightly bitter natural outer coating, and then cooked like the other wholegrains. It can be used like brown rice but has a slightly sweeter taste. The dried grains can be made into flour.

Rye

Rye is perhaps the most important cereal crop in Scandinavia and parts of Central Europe, such as Russia and Germany, and is a hardy alternative to wheat. Rye grains contain relatively little gluten, which is why rye flour doesn't make very good risen yeast bread. However, it does make excellent pumpernickel-type bread and crispbreads that have a good, strong, nutty flavour.

Cracked rye, whole grains of rye cracked so they cook more quickly, is often used in rye bread to add texture.

Rye flakes are similar in appearance to oat flakes. They are wholegrains that have been flattened and often toasted. They can be used in muesli.

Whole rye grains can be cooked like rice, but, as they are very tough when raw, they need to be soaked overnight and then drained before cooking.

whole rye grains

rye flakes

cracked rye

rye flour

quinoa

Spelt

This is an ancient variety of wheat, from which our modern wheat was developed. Wholegrains of spelt can be cooked and used like rice. Spelt flour and spelt pasta are also available. Spelt is higher in iron and B vitamins than modern wheat.

Wheat

Half the world's population relies on wheat as its staple food. First grown as a crop 12,000 years ago in the plains of Mesopotamia, it arrived in Italy around the time of Julius Caesar, in Britain at the time of the Roman invasion, and in the West Indies with Columbus in 1493. Ground into flour, it is the most popular grain for bread-making, but it also has other forms and uses. Wheat contains gluten and is unsuitable for coeliacs.

Bran is the tough outer layer of the grain which is removed in the milling of white flour. The bran contains much of the grain's fibre and is often used as an additive in commercial products to increase a food's overall fibre content.

Bulghur wheat is often referred to as cracked wheat, but is actually a more refined version. It is produced by cooking grains of wheat, which contain all the grain except the bran, until they crack. They are then dried and ground between rollers to either a fine, medium or coarse consistency. Bulghur wheat needs only a few minutes cooking or can be soaked for 15–30 minutes. With its attractive golden appearance and nutty flavour, it is delicious in salads such as tabbouleh and for stuffing aubergines, beef tomatoes and other vegetables.

Cracked wheat is also known as kibbled wheat. Grains of wheat are cut by steel blades or roughly milled to crack the wheat into coarse, medium or fine pieces. It is not pre-cooked so it takes longer to cook than bulghur wheat (and cooks to a stickier texture), but takes less time than wholewheat.

Wheat flakes are whole grains of wheat flattened under rollers to make flakes for adding to muesli, or use in vegetarian burgers, or as part of a savoury crumble topping.

Wheatgerm, the tiny embryo within the seed of wheat that contains much of the nutrient profile of the grain, can be sprinkled on foods such as breakfast cereal or salads. Untreated wheatgerm can quickly go rancid because of its high fat content, and should be kept in the fridge.

Wholewheat grains, or 'berries', can be boiled and used in the same way as brown rice and other wholegrains. Pre-cooked wholewheat is available in many supermarkets.

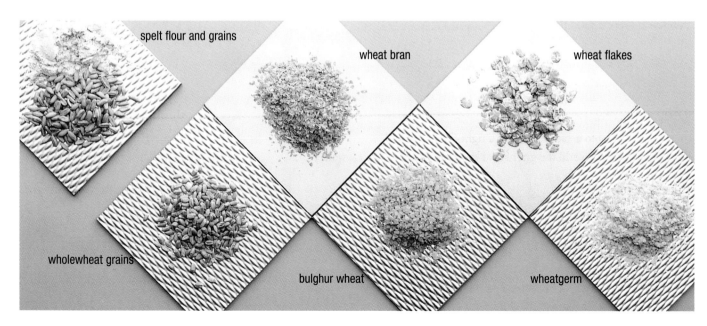

spelt flour and grains

wheat bran

wheat flakes

wholewheat grains

bulghur wheat

wheatgerm

Clockwise from back left: whisky, popcorn, barley wine, bread, couscous, semolina, bread flours

Cooking whole grains

Whole grains – pot barley, whole oats, quinoa, whole rye, spelt and wholewheat – can be cooked like rice, and served as part of a main course or as an accompaniment. Whole rye grains need to be soaked in cold water overnight before cooking. Wholewheat grains, if not pre-cooked, can be soaked overnight to shorten the cooking time.

● Weigh out the grains, allowing about 75 g (2½ oz) per person for part of a main course.

● If the quantity of liquid needed for cooking is not specified on the packet, pour the grains into a measuring jug to check the volume. Then measure out 3 parts water to one part grains (with the exception of millet, which needs 4 parts water).

● Pour the water into a saucepan with a tight-fitting lid and bring to the boil, then add the grains and return to the boil. (Or, add the grains to the water and bring to the boil, according to the recipe or packet instructions.) For extra flavour, stir the grains in a little hot oil or melted butter in the saucepan, to toast them lightly, before adding the water.

● Lower the heat and simmer very gently until all the water has been absorbed, without stirring. Cooking time will vary from grain to grain: millet and quinoa will usually be tender in about 20 minutes; tougher grains may take an hour or more.

● Remove from the heat and leave, with lid on, for a further 10 minutes. By this time the grains should be separate and tender but not mushy. Fork through the grains and serve.

Favourite foods from grains

Grains are used to make many of our favourite foods. Flours and bread are the most commonly known form of processed grains and both are staple foods throughout the world. Flour and bread can be made from almost any grain – cornbread is popular in the Americas, and dark and light rye breads in Eastern Europe. Grains can also be used to make alcoholic beverages such as whisky and barley wine.

● **Semolina** is a processed form of durum wheat, made from the starchy part (endosperm) of the grain. It can be used in milk puddings. Semolina flour is mixed with water, and sometimes egg, to make pasta.

● **Couscous** is made from a mixture of semolina flour and water that is rolled in flour to produce tiny, round, yellow pieces. It is simply soaked or steamed, and then used as an accompaniment or part of a salad or other dish.

● **Popcorn** is made from whole grains of an especially hard variety of corn, which when heated make a popping sound and puff up to quadruple their size.

Soups and Starters

Delicious first courses plus some hearty soups

Put cereal grains and pulses right up front on the menu, in appetising starters and soups. A salad of Puy lentils and flakes of smoked mackerel with a zesty dressing will set tastebuds tingling, as will a spicy Mexican bean soup served with tortillas. For entertaining, make a creamy, olive-studded bean terrine wrapped in vine leaves, or tempt your guests with little rice pancakes topped with fresh crab. Slices of grilled polenta with rich Gorgonzola cheese makes another irresistible starter, as does a beautifully coloured tomato and red rice soup enriched with white wine. Or try an Italian classic, white bean and bacon soup scented with fresh rosemary.

Tomato and red rice soup

This richly flavoured, chunky soup makes a satisfying starter or can be served for lunch with a well-flavoured cheese and some crusty bread. Canned tomatoes have a more intense colour and flavour than most fresh ones, particularly during the colder months, and need no skinning or other preparation for this soup.

Serves 4

2 tbsp extra virgin olive oil
6 shallots, finely chopped
85 g (3 oz) Camargue red rice
150 ml (5 fl oz) dry white wine
400 ml (14 fl oz) vegetable stock
1 can chopped tomatoes, about 400 g
3 tbsp finely chopped fresh oregano or basil
salt and pepper
To serve
4 tbsp crème fraîche
fresh basil or oregano leaves

Preparation time: 10 minutes
Cooking time: 40–45 minutes

1 Heat the oil in a large saucepan, add the shallots and fry gently for 4–5 minutes or until softened.

2 Add the rice and stir to coat all the grains evenly with the oil, then cook gently for 30 seconds. Stir in the wine and boil rapidly for 30 seconds, then add the stock and the tomatoes with their juice.

3 Bring to the boil, then cover and simmer for 35–40 minutes or until the rice is just tender.

4 Stir in the chopped oregano or basil, and season with salt and pepper to taste. Ladle the soup into serving bowls, add 1 tbsp of crème fraîche to each one and top with a few basil leaves. Serve hot.

Another idea

● To make mushroom and rice soup, replace the red rice with 75 g (2½ oz) long-grain white rice and use 75 ml (2½ fl oz) dry sherry instead of the white wine. After adding the sherry in step 2, boil until it has almost all evaporated, then stir in 350 g (12½ oz) finely chopped chestnut or closed-cup mushrooms. Cook for about 2 minutes or until softened. Pour in 750 ml (1¼ pints) chicken stock and 1 tbsp Worcestershire sauce. Cover and simmer gently for 10 minutes. Stir in 1 tbsp chopped fresh tarragon and simmer for a further 5 minutes or until the rice is tender. Serve hot, topping each serving with 1 tbsp soured cream and a few fresh tarragon leaves.

Plus points

● Camargue red rice, from the wetlands of the Camargue region in southern France, is particularly nutritious, having a higher fibre content even than brown rice. Like all varieties of rice, red rice is an excellent ingredient to include in a healthy diet, as it is high in starchy carbohydrate and low in fat.

● Tomatoes, originally known as love apples and once used only as an ornamental plant, are now valued as an important source of vitamin C and beta-carotene, both of which are powerful antioxidants.

Each serving provides Ⓥ

kcal 280, **protein** 3 g, **fat** 18 g (of which saturated fat 8 g), **carbohydrate** 21 g (of which sugars 4 g), **fibre** 1 g

✓✓	A
✓	C, E, calcium, potassium

Tuscan white bean soup

This simple, wholesome soup, typical of the cooking of Tuscany, makes a delicious starter. It is very easy to prepare, although you need to soak the dried beans ahead of time. Should you forget, you can use canned beans to make the quick version suggested in Some more ideas, below. Serve with warm ciabatta or rustic bread.

Serves 4

1 tbsp extra virgin olive oil

2 rashers lean smoked back bacon, rinded and chopped

1 onion, chopped

2 garlic cloves, chopped

1 red pepper, seeded and finely chopped

100 g (3½ oz) dried cannellini beans, soaked for at least 8 hours

1.4 litres (2½ pints) hot chicken or vegetable stock

2 sprigs fresh rosemary or 1 tsp dried rosemary

100 g (3½ oz) Savoy cabbage, finely shredded

salt and pepper

Preparation time: 10 minutes, plus 8 hours soaking

Cooking time: 1½ hours

Each serving provides

kcal 158, **protein** 9 g, **fat** 6 g (of which saturated fat 1 g), **carbohydrate** 19 g (of which sugars 6 g), **fibre** 6 g

✓✓✓ A, C

✓ B₁, B₆, folate, niacin, calcium, copper, iron, potassium, zinc

1 Heat the oil in a large saucepan, add the bacon and onion, and cook gently for 5 minutes or until the onion is softened. Add the garlic and red pepper, and cook gently for a further 2 minutes.

2 Drain the soaked beans and rinse under cold running water. Add them to the pan together with the stock. Bring to the boil and boil rapidly for 10 minutes, then reduce the heat so the liquid is simmering. Skim off any froth.

3 Add the rosemary. Partly cover the pan and simmer for 45–60 minutes or until the beans are very tender.

4 Remove about 3 tbsp of the beans with a draining spoon, place them in a basin and mash with a fork.

5 Add the cabbage to the soup and simmer for 5 minutes. Remove the rosemary twigs, if using fresh rosemary, then stir the mashed beans into the soup to thicken it slightly. Season with salt and pepper to taste, and serve hot.

Some more ideas

• For a very quick version of this soup, use 1 can cannellini beans, about 410 g, drained and rinsed, instead of dried beans. Cook the vegetables and bacon as in the main recipe, then add 1.2 litres (2 pints) stock and the rosemary, and bring to the boil. Add the beans and simmer gently for 5 minutes, to heat the beans through. Continue from step 4 as above.

• You can substitute dried haricot beans for the cannellini beans.

• For a flageolet bean soup, replace the cannellini beans with dried flageolet beans. Soften the onion and garlic in the olive oil with 2 finely chopped celery sticks (omit the bacon and red pepper). Add the beans and the stock. Bring to the boil, then add 1 tbsp pesto sauce instead of the rosemary. Simmer for 45–60 minutes or until the beans are very tender. Remove about 3 tbsp of the beans and mash them. Instead of cabbage, add 100 g (3½ oz) frozen peas to the soup. Bring back to the boil and simmer for 3–4 minutes, then add 85 g (3 oz) baby spinach leaves and the grated zest of 1 lemon. Simmer for 1 minute or until the spinach has wilted. Stir the mashed beans into the soup, season to taste and serve.

Plus points

• Dried beans are an excellent source of soluble fibre, which can help to reduce high blood cholesterol levels.

• Savoy cabbage, one of the hardiest of all cabbages, is easily recognized by its crinkly leaves. It contains a number of different phytochemicals that appear to help reduce the risk of cancer.

Winter pumpkin and rice soup

This is a hearty, warming soup, perfect for cold, damp winter days. When puréed, the pumpkin and rice become silken smooth, giving the soup a velvety texture. Just a little curry powder is all you need to add a touch of subtle heat. This soup makes a tempting and filling starter.

Serves 6

1 kg (2¼ lb) pumpkin
2 tbsp extra virgin olive oil
2 onions, chopped
1 tsp mild curry powder
2 garlic cloves, finely chopped
1 fresh, hot green chilli, seeded and finely chopped
1 litre (1¾ pints) vegetable stock
175 g (6¼ oz) risotto rice
a little hot vegetable stock (optional)
1 tbsp chopped fresh coriander
salt and pepper

Preparation time: 20 minutes
Cooking time: 40–45 minutes

Each serving provides   Ⓥ

kcal 179, protein 4 g, fat 5 g (of which saturated fat 1 g), carbohydrate 30 g (of which sugars 6 g), fibre 2.5 g

✓✓	C
✓	A, B₁, E, copper, potassium, zinc

1 Peel the pumpkin and remove the seeds and fibres from the centre. Rinse the seeds and reserve. Cut the pumpkin flesh into cubes.

2 Heat the oil in a large saucepan, add the onions and curry powder, and cook over a low to moderate heat, stirring frequently, for 15–20 minutes or until the onions soften and start to caramelise.

3 Add the cubes of pumpkin, the garlic and chilli, and stir to coat with the onion mixture. Pour in the stock and add 5 tbsp of the rice. Bring to the boil, then cover the pan, reduce the heat and simmer for 25 minutes or until the pumpkin and rice are very soft.

4 Meanwhile, bring a saucepan of water to the boil, add the remaining rice and simmer for about 15 minutes or until just tender. Drain in a sieve, rinse lightly under cold water and leave to drain again.

5 Preheat the grill to moderately high. Spread out the pumpkin seeds on a baking sheet in a single layer and toast under the grill for 3–5 minutes or until golden and aromatic, turning them several times. Set aside.

6 When the pumpkin and rice are soft, purée the soup, either in a blender or food processor, or using a hand-held blender directly in the pan.

7 Stir in the cooked rice and season with salt and pepper to taste. Reheat gently. If the soup seems too thick, stir in a little hot vegetable stock or water. Stir in the chopped coriander and serve, sprinkled with the toasted pumpkin seeds.

Plus points

- Pumpkin is one of the largest winter squashes and can be used as a vegetable or in sweet dishes such as the traditional American dessert for Thanksgiving, pumpkin pie. Pumpkin is rich in beta-carotene, as well as other antioxidants such as lutein and zeaxanthin, all of which can help to protect the body against infections and diseases.
- Rice is the most important cereal grain in the world, with some 2,500 varieties. It is a source of protein, starchy carbohydrate and most B vitamins. These, with the addition of vitamins from the pumpkin, make this a very nutritious soup.

Some more ideas

● Replace the curry powder with 1 tbsp dried rosemary or dried mixed herbs.

● To make butternut squash, apple and rice soup, use butternut squash instead of pumpkin, preparing it in the same way but without reserving and toasting the seeds. Caramelise the onions in the oil, flavouring with ground cumin instead of curry powder. Add the squash to the pan with 1 peeled, cored and diced cooking apple and 2 chopped garlic cloves, then add the stock and 85 g (3 oz) basmati rice. Simmer as in the main recipe, at the same time cooking another 85 g (3 oz) basmati rice in water in a separate pan. Peel and core 1 tart eating apple and cut into small cubes. Sauté in 15 g (½ oz) butter for about 5 minutes or until tender. Purée the soup as in the main recipe, then stir in the cooked rice and sautéed apple. Finish by stirring in 1 tbsp Calvados and 2 tbsp crème fraîche.

Mexican black-eyed bean soup

The creamy texture of black-eyed beans works particularly well in warming, spicy soups. This one is filling enough to make a hearty main course. A scattering of grated cheese melting into the soup is the finishing touch.

Serves 6

1 tbsp sunflower oil

1 large fresh green chilli, seeded and finely chopped

2 green peppers, seeded and chopped

1 tsp ground cumin

1 can chopped tomatoes, about 400 g

1 tsp sun-dried tomato paste

600–750 ml (1–1¼ pints) vegetable stock

1 bay leaf

2 cans black-eyed beans, about 410 g each, drained and rinsed

170 g (6 oz) frozen sweetcorn

3 tbsp chopped fresh coriander

salt and pepper

To serve

12 large flour tortillas

85 g (3 oz) Monterey Jack cheese, coarsely grated

sprigs of fresh coriander (optional)

thinly sliced fresh green chilli (optional)

Preparation time: 20 minutes

Cooking time: 20 minutes

1 Heat the oil in a large saucepan, add the chilli and green peppers, and cook gently for 5 minutes or until almost soft, stirring frequently. Stir in the ground cumin and cook for a few seconds longer.

2 Add the canned tomatoes with their juice, the tomato paste, 600 ml (1 pint) of the stock, the bay leaf and 1½ cans of the beans. Bring slowly to the boil, then turn down the heat, cover and simmer gently for 15 minutes. Discard the bay leaf.

3 Purée the soup, either in batches in a blender or food processor, or using a hand-held blender directly in the pan. Stir in the remaining beans, plus the sweetcorn and chopped coriander. Add enough of the remaining 150 ml (5 fl oz) stock to thin the soup to the desired consistency. Season with salt and pepper to taste, then heat through gently until piping hot.

4 Meanwhile, heat the tortillas in the oven or microwave, according to the packet instructions.

5 Ladle the soup into bowls and sprinkle over the cheese. Garnish with coriander sprigs and green chilli, if liked. Serve with the tortillas.

Plus points

● Using canned beans rather than dried beans has little effect on the nutritional value of a dish, and it certainly saves time. Though an excellent source of dietary fibre, beans can produce unpleasant side effects, such as wind and bloating. Rinsing canned beans thoroughly can help to remove some of the sugars that cause these problems.

● Monterey Jack cheese is a hard cheese made from cow's milk, not unlike Cheddar though with a blander flavour. Like other hard cheeses, it is an excellent source of calcium as well as protein.

Each serving provides Ⓥ

kcal 438, **protein** 19 g, **fat** 9 g (of which saturated fat 3.5 g), **carbohydrate** 75 g (of which sugars 6 g), **fibre** 7 g

✓✓✓ C, folate
✓✓ B_1, E, copper, iron, zinc
✓ A, B_6, niacin, calcium, potassium, selenium

Some more ideas

● If you can't find Monterey Jack cheese, use Wensleydale or mild Cheddar instead.

● Substitute canned pinto or black beans for black-eyed beans.

● For a roasted vegetable and kidney bean soup, peel, seed and cube ½ butternut squash, about 350 g (12½ oz). Put on a baking tray with 1 halved onion, 1 halved parsnip and 1 thickly sliced leek. Drizzle over 1 tbsp extra virgin olive oil and toss to coat, then tuck 2 sprigs of fresh thyme under the vegetables. Roast in a preheated 200ºC (400ºF, gas mark 6) oven for 45 minutes or until the vegetables are tender, turning occasionally so they brown evenly. Add 4 rinded rashers of smoked back bacon for the last 15 minutes of the cooking time. Set the bacon aside to cool; discard the thyme and any fat from the bacon, then tip the vegetables into a saucepan. Mix in 1 can red kidney beans, about 410 g, drained and rinsed, and 900 ml (1½ pints) vegetable stock. Purée with a hand-held blender (or in a blender or food processor), then stir in a second can of drained and rinsed red kidney beans and season. Heat thoroughly, then ladle into bowls and swirl 1 tsp pesto in each. Crumble the bacon and scatter on top.

Red lentil and celery soup with melted Stilton and chives

Carrots give a slightly sweet edge to this thick, smooth soup, which contains delicious pockets of melted blue cheese. All you need with it is some crusty bread to make a satisfying and nutritious main course.

Serves 4

1½ tbsp extra virgin olive oil

1 large mild onion, roughly chopped

300 g (10½ oz) split red lentils

1.7 litres (3 pints) well-flavoured vegetable stock

4 large carrots, about 400 g (14 oz), sliced

1 head of celery, about 500 g (1 lb 2 oz), sliced, some of the leaves reserved for garnish

100 g (3½ oz) Stilton cheese, crumbled

4 tbsp snipped fresh chives

salt and pepper

Preparation time: 15 minutes

Cooking time: about 1 hour

Each serving provides ⓥ

kcal 444, **protein** 25 g, **fat** 15 g (of which saturated fat 6 g), **carbohydrate** 56 g (of which sugars 14 g), **fibre** 8 g

✓✓✓	A, copper
✓✓	B₁, B₆, niacin, calcium, iron, potassium, zinc
✓	B₂, C, E, folate, selenium

1 Heat the oil in a large saucepan, add the onion, and cook gently, stirring occasionally, for 10 minutes or until softened.

2 Tip the lentils into the pan and pour in the vegetable stock. Bring to the boil. Add the carrots and celery. Bring back to the boil, then cover and simmer for about 40 minutes or until the lentils and vegetables are very tender.

3 Purée the soup, either in a blender or food processor, or using a hand-held blender directly in the pan. Season with salt and pepper to taste. Reheat until the soup is piping hot, but not boiling. Remove from the heat.

4 Scatter the crumbled Stilton over the soup and stir in the chives. Ladle into soup bowls, garnish with the celery leaves and serve.

Another idea

• Make a red lentil and caramelised onion soup. Cook 500 g (1 lb 2 oz) thinly sliced mild onions with 4 sliced garlic cloves in 3 tbsp extra virgin olive oil for 10 minutes or until softened. Sprinkle over 2 tsp caster sugar and fry for a further 15 minutes or until the onions are golden and caramelised. Add 300 g (10½ oz) split red lentils, 1.7 litres (3 pints) vegetable stock, 300 ml (10 fl oz) dry white wine, 1 tsp

crushed black peppercorns and 4 bay leaves. Simmer for 40 minutes or until the lentils are tender, then remove the bay leaves. Purée half of the soup, then stir this back into the rest of the soup in the pan. Season and reheat. Serve with cheese croûtes, made while the soup is simmering: arrange 12 slices of baguette in clusters of 3 on a foil-lined grill pan. Sprinkle with 85 g (3 oz) grated Gruyère cheese and grill until the cheese melts and starts to turn golden (the cheese will stick the bread slices together). Ladle the soup into soup plates. Carefully place 3 cheese croûte clusters on top of each portion and serve immediately.

Plus points

• Unlike other pulses, lentils do not need to be soaked before cooking. They are a good source of protein, starchy carbohydrate, fibre and B vitamins.

• Celery has only been used as a vegetable and salad ingredient since the late 17th century. It contains potassium, a mineral that helps to regulate fluid balance in the body, and therefore helps in the prevention of high blood pressure. It also contains a compound called phthalide, which may aid in lowering blood pressure.

Greek-style lemon chicken soup

This delicate yet rich-tasting soup is packed with good things, and makes a warming and sustaining main course. Chicken breasts are poached with vegetables, then rice is cooked in the well-flavoured stock. At the last minute, the soup is enriched with eggs and fresh lemon juice in traditional Greek fashion.

Serves 4

3 small skinless boneless chicken breasts (fillets), about 340 g (12 oz) in total

1 large onion, thinly sliced

2 celery sticks, chopped

1 large carrot, thinly sliced

6 black peppercorns

strip of lemon zest

1 small bunch of fresh dill or flat-leaf parsley

150 g (5½ oz) long-grain white rice

juice of 1 lemon

2 eggs, beaten

salt and pepper

sprigs of fresh dill or flat-leaf parsley to garnish

Preparation time: 15 minutes
Cooking time: 30 minutes

Each serving provides

kcal 305, **protein** 28 g, **fat** 5 g (of which saturated fat 1 g), **carbohydrate** 40 g (of which sugars 6 g), **fibre** 2 g

✓✓✓	A, niacin
✓✓	B₆, selenium
✓	B₁, B₂, B₁₂, C, folate, copper, iron, potassium, zinc

1 Put the chicken breasts, onion, celery, carrot, black peppercorns, lemon zest and bunch of dill or parsley into a large saucepan. Add 1.4 litres (2½ pints) water. Bring to the boil over a moderate heat, skimming off any foam that comes to the surface. Reduce the heat and half-cover the pan with a lid, so the water just bubbles gently. Simmer for 15 minutes or until the chicken is cooked through.

2 Remove the chicken from the pan with a draining spoon and set aside. Strain the stock through a large sieve into a clean pan, discarding the vegetables and flavourings.

3 Reheat the stock until boiling, then stir in the rice. Simmer gently for 8–10 minutes or until the rice is almost tender. Meanwhile, cut or tear the chicken into thin shreds, and mix the lemon juice with the beaten eggs.

4 Add the shredded chicken to the soup. Heat over a moderate heat until the soup almost starts to boil again. Remove the pan from the heat and pour in the lemon juice mixture, stirring constantly. Season with salt and pepper to taste. Serve immediately, garnished with sprigs of dill or parsley.

Another idea

• Try Chinese-style duck and rice soup. Replace the chicken with 2 medium-sized skinless duck breasts, about 300 g (10½ oz) in total. Instead of lemon zest and dill or parsley, flavour the stock with 4 slices of fresh root ginger (no need to peel it) and the stalks from a small bunch of fresh coriander. Simmer for 20 minutes, then remove the duck and shred. Strain the stock, then reheat with 1 tsp grated fresh root ginger. Add 2 thinly sliced celery sticks and 85 g (3 oz) long-grain white rice. When the rice is almost cooked, add the shredded duck, 1 tbsp chopped fresh coriander, a pinch of crushed dried chillies and a dash of soy sauce to taste. Bring back to the boil, then serve immediately.

Plus points

• The combination of rice, lean chicken and vegetables keeps this soup low in fat, while providing good amounts of protein and starchy carbohydrate.

• Although eggs contain cholesterol, it is now generally agreed that, for most people, eating them has little effect on blood cholesterol levels. Rather, it is the intake of saturated fat, as well as other factors, that can increase blood cholesterol. As eggs are an excellent source of protein, they can make a valuable contribution to a healthy diet.

Garlicky flageolet bean terrine

Wrapped in shining green vine leaves and studded with stuffed green olives, this creamy terrine is a real winner. It is made with tender flageolet beans and curd cheese, and subtly flavoured with garlic. Serve it with crisp chicory leaves, fresh orange segments and crusty French bread for an unusual and attractive starter.

Serves 8

225 g (8 oz) dried flageolet beans, soaked for at least 8 hours

1 small onion, halved

strip of lemon zest

2 bay leaves

10 vine leaves preserved in brine, or as needed

115 g (4 oz) curd cheese

2 garlic cloves, crushed

1 tbsp lemon juice

2 eggs, lightly beaten

2 tbsp chopped parsley

50 g (1¾ oz) pimiento-stuffed green olives, sliced

salt and pepper

To serve

1 small head chicory, leaves separated

2 oranges, peeled and segmented

45 g (1½ oz) toasted almonds

Preparation and cooking time: 2¾ hours, plus 6–8 hours soaking and 2 hours chilling

Each serving provides　　　　　Ⓥ

kcal 177, **protein** 13 g, **fat** 8 g (of which saturated fat 2 g), **carbohydrate** 15 g (of which sugars 6 g), **fibre** 9 g

✓✓✓	copper
✓✓	C
✓	A, B₁, B₂, B₁₂, E, niacin, calcium, iron, potassium, zinc

1 Drain the soaked beans and rinse under cold running water. Put them in a saucepan with the onion, lemon zest, bay leaves and enough cold water to cover generously. Bring to the boil and boil rapidly for 10 minutes, then reduce the heat and simmer for 45–60 minutes or until tender.

2 Meanwhile, drain the vine leaves and rinse them in cold water. Spread out on kitchen paper and pat dry. Lightly oil a 900 g (2 lb) terrine dish or loaf tin and line it with the vine leaves, shiny side out, allowing them to hang over the top of the dish. Set aside.

3 Preheat the oven to 180°C (350°F, gas mark 4). Drain the beans and discard the onion, lemon zest and bay leaves. Tip the beans into a bowl and mash with a potato masher until fairly smooth.

4 Add the curd cheese, garlic, lemon juice, eggs, parsley, and salt and pepper to taste. Mix together, then fold in the olives. Spoon into the prepared terrine dish or tin, pressing the mixture into the corners. Level the top, then fold over the overhanging leaves. Cover with additional leaves, if necessary.

5 Cover the top of the dish or tin with a piece of oiled foil, tucking the edges under the rim to seal securely. Set the dish in a roasting tin and pour in enough warm water to come two-thirds of the way up the sides of the dish. Bake for 1 hour or until the top of the terrine feels firm to the touch. Remove the dish from the water, set it on a wire rack and leave to cool. Chill for at least 2 hours before serving.

6 To unmould, run a knife round the edges of the terrine and turn out onto a plate or board. Cut into slices and transfer to plates. Garnish each portion with chicory leaves, orange segments and almonds, and serve.

Plus points

● Flageolet beans are packed with protein, soluble fibre and starchy carbohydrate. They also contain useful amounts of iron.

● Curd cheese is made with a lactic acid starter, which gives it a fresh, slightly sharp flavour. It contains about half the amount of fat of hard cheeses such as Cheddar.

soups and starters

Some more ideas

• The flageolet bean mixture also makes a delicious dip. Omit the eggs, and stir in 1 tbsp extra virgin olive oil and an extra 1 tsp lemon juice. Spoon into a serving bowl and serve with vegetable crudités and breadsticks.

• For an aduki bean and leek terrine, soak 225 g (8 oz) dried aduki beans for 8 hours, then drain and rinse. Put in a saucepan with fresh water to cover and add 2 bay leaves and a strip of orange zest. Bring to the boil and boil rapidly for 10 minutes, then reduce the heat and simmer for about 45 minutes or until tender. Drain, reserving 4 tbsp of the cooking liquid. Discard the bay leaves and orange zest, and purée or mash the beans with the reserved liquid until as smooth as possible. Mix in 115 g (4 oz) curd cheese, 55 g (2 oz) chopped toasted hazelnuts, 2 beaten eggs, 1 crushed garlic clove, 2 tbsp chopped fresh tarragon, and seasoning. Cook 225 g (8 oz) baby leeks in boiling water for 2 minutes, then drain and refresh in cold water. Pat dry on kitchen paper. Line the terrine dish or loaf tin with baking parchment, then spoon in one-quarter of the bean mixture. Arrange a third of the leeks on top, trimming them to fit if necessary. Repeat the layers, finishing with the bean mixture. Cover and bake as in the main recipe. Serve garnished with green salad leaves.

Smoked mackerel and Puy lentil salad with lime dressing

Large flakes of peppered smoked mackerel, sprigs of watercress and thick slices of juicy, sweet pear make an exciting combination, and they work well with earthy, nutty-textured Puy lentils in a lime and honey dressing. Serve with Melba toast or wholemeal bread for a starter that will set tastebuds tingling.

Serves 6

140 g (5 oz) Puy lentils

150 g (5½ oz) peppered smoked mackerel fillet, skinned and flaked into large pieces

3 spring onions, thinly sliced on the diagonal

85 g (3 oz) watercress sprigs

1 large pear, preferably red-skinned, cored and thickly sliced

Lime dressing

2 tbsp extra virgin olive oil

grated zest and juice of 1 lime

1 tsp Dijon mustard

1 tbsp clear honey

salt and pepper

Preparation and cooking time: 25–30 minutes

Each serving provides

kcal 222, protein 11 g, fat 12 g (of which saturated fat 2 g), carbohydrate 18 g (of which sugars 7 g), fibre 3 g

✓✓✓	B₁₂, selenium
✓✓	C, copper
✓	A, B₁, B₆, niacin, iron, potassium, zinc

1 Put the lentils into a saucepan, cover with cold water and bring to the boil. Reduce the heat and simmer for 15–20 minutes or until they are tender but slightly firm to the bite.

2 Meanwhile, make the dressing. Put the olive oil, lime zest and juice, mustard and honey in a mixing bowl, and add salt and pepper to taste. Whisk together well.

3 Drain the lentils and tip into the mixing bowl. Toss to coat with the dressing, then fold in the mackerel and spring onions.

4 Arrange the watercress and pear slices on 6 serving plates. Spoon the lentil and mackerel mixture on top and serve immediately.

Another idea

● To make a smoked trout and green lentil salad with raspberry vinaigrette, replace the Puy lentils with green lentils, cooking them for 20–30 minutes. In the dressing, replace the lime zest and juice with 2 tbsp raspberry vinegar. Instead of smoked mackerel, fold in large flakes of smoked trout. Spoon the lentil mixture onto a bed of 85 g (3 oz) watercress tossed with 45 g (1½ oz) torn Lollo Rosso leaves and garnish with 55 g (2 oz) raspberries.

Plus points

● Although lentils contain iron, the absorption of this mineral from them is normally poor. Adding ingredients rich in vitamin C, such as limes and watercress, can improve the absorption of iron considerably.

● Oily fish such as mackerel (both fresh and smoked) are rich in omega-3 fatty acids, a type of polyunsaturated fat that is believed to help to prevent heart disease and strokes by making the blood less sticky and therefore less likely to clot. Omega-3 fats may also be helpful in preventing and treating arthritis.

● Dark green, leafy vegetables such as watercress provide many vitamins and minerals, including beta-carotene, vitamin C and folate. Watercress is also a good source of calcium.

Dolmades

Here's a new, healthy twist on these delicious and popular little Greek parcels. To boost the fibre and nutrient content, brown rice is used instead of the traditional white. The filling for the vine leaves is flavoured with garlic and fresh herbs, with a hint of sweetness from raisins and crunch from walnuts.

Serves 8 (makes 24)

200 g (7 oz) long-grain brown rice

24 large vine leaves preserved in brine, about
   115 g (4 oz) in total when drained

3 tbsp extra virgin olive oil

1 onion, finely chopped

1 large garlic clove, finely chopped

1 tbsp chopped parsley

1 tbsp chopped fresh mint

1 tbsp chopped fresh dill

grated zest and juice of 1 lemon

50 g (1¾ oz) raisins

50 g (1¾ oz) walnuts, chopped

salt and pepper

To garnish

lemon wedges

sprigs of fresh dill, parsley or mint

Preparation time: 1 hour
Cooking time: 10–15 minutes

Each serving provides   Ⓥ

kcal 199, **protein** 4 g, **fat** 9 g (of which saturated fat 1 g), **carbohydrate** 27 g (of which sugars 6 g), **fibre** 1 g

✓✓✓ copper

✓   A, B₁, C, folate, calcium, iron, zinc

1 Put the rice in a saucepan and add 600 ml (1 pint) water. Bring to the boil. Stir, then cover with a tight-fitting lid and simmer very gently for 30–40 minutes or until the rice is tender and has absorbed all the water. Remove from the heat.

2 While the rice is cooking, drain the vine leaves, rinse with cold water and pat dry with kitchen paper.

3 Heat 2 tbsp of the oil in a saucepan over a moderate heat. Add the onion and garlic, and cook, stirring occasionally, for 5–8 minutes or until soft but not browned. Remove from the heat and stir in the parsley, mint, dill, lemon zest and raisins.

4 Put the walnuts in a small frying pan and toast them over a moderate heat, stirring constantly, until lightly browned and aromatic.

5 Add the toasted walnuts to the onion mixture. Stir in the cooked rice and add the lemon juice (you may not need all of it), and salt and pepper to taste. Mix well.

6 Spread one of the vine leaves flat on a work surface and place about 2 spoonfuls of the rice mixture in the centre. Fold over the stalk end, then fold in the sides. Roll up the leaf into a cylinder shape. Repeat with the remaining vine leaves and filling.

7 Place the rolls seam side down in a steamer and brush the tops with the remaining 1 tbsp olive oil. Cover and steam for 10–15 minutes or until piping hot. Serve hot or at room temperature, garnished with lemon wedges and sprigs of fresh herbs.

Plus points

• Brown rice has only the outer husk removed and therefore contains all the nutrients in the germ and outer layers of the grain. Raw brown rice contains 1.9 g fibre per 100 g (3½ oz) compared with 0.4 g fibre for the same weight of raw white rice. It also contains more B vitamins.

• Walnuts are high in unsaturated fats, especially linoleic acid. Recent studies have suggested that regular consumption of walnuts may help to protect against heart attacks.

• Raisins, currants and sultanas are all types of dried grapes. They are rich in sugars, mostly as glucose and fructose, and a useful source of iron, potassium and fibre.

Another idea

● To make stuffed cabbage rolls, use 12 large Savoy cabbage leaves instead of the vine leaves. Blanch them for 1 minute in boiling water, then refresh under cold running water and pat dry. Cut out the tough cores. Cook the onion and garlic as in the main recipe, then add 1 tbsp chopped fresh thyme, the grated zest of 1 orange and 50 g (1¾ oz) each chopped dried apricots and chopped toasted almonds. Stir in the rice and the juice of ½ orange, and season with salt and pepper to taste. Roll up the filling in the cabbage leaves as instructed for the vine leaves. Make a simple tomato sauce by combining 2 tbsp extra virgin olive oil, 1 finely chopped onion and 1 can chopped tomatoes, about 400 g, with the juice, in a saucepan and simmering for 15–20 minutes or until the onion is soft and the sauce slightly thickened. Season to taste, then pour into a shallow baking dish. Place the cabbage rolls on top, seam side down, and cover the dish with foil. Bake in a preheated 180ºC (350ºF, gas mark 4) oven for 25 minutes or until piping hot.

Herb and saffron risotto

This fragrant, fresh-tasting risotto can be served either as a starter or as a side dish. It should be eaten as soon as it is cooked – if it is left to stand, the starch will begin to set, resulting in a heavy texture. Lemon zest and juice and fresh herbs stirred in at the end add a wonderful burst of flavour.

Serves 6

15 g (½ oz) butter

2 tbsp extra virgin olive oil

1 small onion, chopped

340 g (12 oz) risotto rice

150 ml (5 fl oz) dry white wine

small pinch of saffron strands

1.5 litres (2¾ pints) hot vegetable stock

grated zest of 1 lemon

2 tbsp lemon juice

2 tbsp chopped fresh chives

2 tbsp chopped parsley

salt and pepper

To serve

15 g (½ oz) Parmesan cheese

snipped fresh chives

Preparation time: 10 minutes

Cooking time: about 25 minutes

1 Heat the butter and oil in a large saucepan, add the onion and cook gently for 4–5 minutes or until softened, stirring from time to time.

2 Add the rice and cook for 1 minute, stirring to coat all the grains with the butter and oil. Stir in the wine and boil until it has almost all evaporated.

3 Stir the saffron into the hot stock. Add a ladleful of the stock to the pan and bubble gently until it has almost all been absorbed, stirring frequently. Continue adding the stock a ladleful at a time, letting each be almost all absorbed before adding the next, and stirring frequently. Total cooking time will be 15–20 minutes. The risotto is ready when the rice is tender but the grains are still whole and firm, and the overall texture is moist and creamy.

4 Remove the pan from the heat and stir in the lemon zest and juice, chives and parsley. Season with salt and pepper to taste.

5 Using a vegetable peeler, take thin shavings from the Parmesan and scatter them over the risotto together with the chives. Serve immediately.

Some more ideas

• Stir 100 g (3½ oz) lightly cooked asparagus tips or thawed frozen peas into the risotto towards the end of cooking.

• To make an artichoke risotto, omit the onion and cook the rice as in the main recipe, adding 2 tbsp lemon juice with the wine. A few minutes before the end of cooking, stir in 1 jar or can of artichoke hearts in water, about 340 g, drained. Add mint instead of parsley, and sprinkle with 30 g (1 oz) chopped walnuts instead of the Parmesan shavings.

Plus points

• Vitamin loss from rice is reduced when it is cooked by the absorption method, as in making a risotto – the vitamins remain in the liquid, which is then absorbed into the dish.

• Parmesan cheese is a very hard cheese made from unpasteurised skimmed cow's milk. It has a high fat content but, as it also has a strong, full taste, only a small amount is needed to add lots of flavour.

Each serving provides Ⓥ

kcal 287, **protein** 6 g, **fat** 7 g (of which saturated fat 2 g), **carbohydrate** 44 g (of which sugars 1 g), **fibre** 0.2 g

✓ niacin, copper, zinc

Rice pancakes with creamy crab

These savoury American-style pancakes have cooked rice included in the batter, which adds an interesting texture and increases their carbohydrate content. They're finished with a quick and delicious fresh crab topping flavoured with dill and a garnish of lumpfish roe. They make a substantial starter or light lunch.

Serves 6 (makes 18)

75 g (2½ oz) long-grain white rice

170 g (6 oz) plain flour

pinch of salt

1 tsp bicarbonate of soda

1 tsp cream of tartar

2 eggs

150 ml (5 fl oz) semi-skimmed milk

1½ tbsp sunflower oil

Crab topping

3 tbsp soured cream

170 g (6 oz) fresh white crab meat

2 tbsp chopped fresh dill

pepper

To serve

1 jar red lumpfish roe, about 55 g

sprigs of fresh dill

lime wedges

Preparation and cooking time: 45 minutes

Each serving provides

kcal 284, protein 14 g, fat 11 g (of which saturated fat 3 g), **carbohydrate** 35 g (of which sugars 2 g), **fibre** 1 g

✓✓✓	copper
✓✓	zinc
✓	A, B₂, B₁₂, E, niacin, calcium, iron, potassium, selenium

1 Put the rice in a pan, add 180 ml (6 fl oz) water and bring to the boil. Stir, then cover and simmer gently for 10–15 minutes or until the rice is tender and has absorbed all the water. Remove from the heat and leave to cool slightly.

2 Sift the flour, salt, bicarbonate of soda and cream of tartar into a mixing bowl. Stir in the rice and make a well in the centre. Lightly beat the eggs and milk together, then add to the well and mix to a thick, smooth batter.

3 Heat a little of the oil in a large, heavy-based, non-stick frying pan. Drop 4 or 5 dessertspoonfuls of the batter into the pan, spaced well apart. Spread each one out slightly with the back of the spoon to about 7.5 cm (3 in) in diameter. Cook over a fairly high heat for 2–3 minutes or until bubbles appear on the tops of the pancakes and they are golden brown underneath.

4 Carefully turn the pancakes over with a palette knife or fish slice and cook the other side for about 2 minutes or until golden. Lift onto a warmed plate, cover loosely with foil and keep warm in a very low oven while cooking the rest of the pancakes.

5 For the topping, gently heat the soured cream in a small saucepan until it begins to bubble. Add the crab meat and stir over a very low heat for

1–2 minutes or until the mixture is just hot. Stir in the chopped dill and season with pepper to taste.

6 Place the pancakes on 6 serving plates. Divide the crab mixture among the pancakes, piling it up in the centre, and garnish each with a little lumpfish roe and a sprig of fresh dill. Add lime wedges to squeeze over and serve immediately.

Plus points

- Polishing the grains to produce white rice removes some of the B vitamins. However, in this recipe the milk, eggs and crab meat make up for this vitamin loss.
- Crab meat is a good source of low-fat protein. It also provides useful amounts of phosphorus, a mineral important for ensuring healthy bones and teeth.
- Milk is rich in many nutrients, the majority of them concentrated in the non-fat part of the milk.

soups and starters

52

Some more ideas

- To give the pancakes a bit of colour contrast, try long-grain brown rice or Camargue red rice, both of which will require 30–35 minutes cooking and 240 ml (8 fl oz) water.
- For an onion and spinach topping, gently cook 1 very thinly sliced onion in 15 g (½ oz) butter and 1 tsp extra virgin olive oil for about 10 minutes. Add 1 crushed garlic clove and cook for a further 5–8 minutes, stirring frequently, until the onion is beginning to caramelise. Meanwhile, cook 170 g (6 oz) baby spinach leaves in a covered pan, with just the water clinging to the leaves after washing, for 3–4 minutes or until wilted. Squeeze out excess water, then add to the onions and cook for about 1 minute to dry slightly. Stir in 2 tbsp crème fraîche and season to taste with freshly grated nutmeg, salt and pepper. Cook briefly until hot, then spoon on top of the pancakes and garnish with finely diced tomato.

Herbed polenta with Gorgonzola

Grilled slices of polenta topped with a creamy, melting mixture of Gorgonzola and ricotta cheeses is a delicious dish, ideal for a tempting starter. It is served hot with a garnish of mixed salad leaves.

Serves 4

750 ml (1¼ pints) vegetable stock

170 g (6 oz) instant polenta

2 tbsp chopped fresh flat-leaf parsley

1 tbsp chopped fresh oregano or marjoram

115 g (4 oz) Gorgonzola cheese

115 g (4 oz) ricotta cheese

1 tbsp extra virgin olive oil

salt and pepper

mixed salad leaves to garnish

Preparation time: 20 minutes, plus 1 hour cooling

Cooking time: 10–15 minutes

1 Bring the stock to the boil in a saucepan. Add the polenta in a steady stream, stirring constantly, and cook for about 5 minutes, or according to the packet instructions, until the mixture has thickened and is pulling away from the sides of the pan.

2 Stir in the parsley and oregano or marjoram, and season with salt and pepper to taste. Pour the polenta onto a greased baking tray and spread out to make a rectangle about 20 x 18 cm (8 x 7½ in) and 1 cm (½ in) thick. Leave in a cool place to set for about 1 hour.

3 Preheat the grill to high. In a bowl, mash the Gorgonzola with the ricotta cheese and set aside. Brush the top of the polenta lightly with the oil, then cut into 12 rectangles, each about 5 x 6 cm (2 x 2½ in). Place on the rack of the grill pan, oiled side up, and grill for 8–10 minutes or until the tops are lightly browned.

4 Turn the polenta slices over and top with the Gorgonzola mixture. Grill for a further 2–3 minutes or until the cheese has melted and is beginning to brown. Serve immediately, garnished with mixed salad leaves.

Some more ideas

● Substitute other herbs such as rosemary, basil or sage for the oregano or marjoram.

● For grilled polenta with sautéed leeks and herbs, make the polenta mixture without the herbs. Melt 45 g (1½ oz) butter in a pan, add 2 finely chopped leeks and 2 crushed garlic cloves, and cook over a moderate heat for about 10 minutes or until soft, stirring occasionally. Stir in 3 tbsp dry sherry and simmer briefly, then stir in 2–3 tbsp chopped fresh mixed herbs and season to taste. Grill the polenta slices for 5–10 minutes on each side, then top with the hot leek mixture and serve.

Plus points

● Like wheat and other grains, maize – from which polenta is made – is rich in starchy carbohydrate and low in fat.

● Gorgonzola is a semi-hard, blue-veined cheese with a rich, full flavour, whereas ricotta is much milder, and lower in fat. Mixing the two cheeses together helps to keep the total fat content of this dish healthy.

Each serving provides

kcal 327, **protein** 12 g, **fat** 15 g (of which saturated fat 8 g), **carbohydrate** 35 g (of which sugars 0.5 g), **fibre** 4 g

✓✓	A, calcium
✓	B₂, zinc

Rice croquettes with mozzarella

Called *suppli* in Italy, these little rice croquettes are based on a classic risotto mixture, which is moulded round nuggets of mozzarella and rolled in breadcrumbs before cooking. It's a great way to use up leftover risotto. Traditionally the croquettes are deep-fried, but here they are baked for a modern streamlined version.

Serves 4 (makes 8)

1 tbsp extra virgin olive oil

1 small onion, finely chopped

200 g (7 oz) risotto rice

3 tbsp dry vermouth

600 ml (1 pint) hot vegetable stock

1 egg, beaten

30 g (1 oz) Parmesan cheese, freshly grated

55 g (2 oz) fine white breadcrumbs, made
from bread 1–2 days old

55 g (2 oz) mozzarella cheese, cut into
8 cubes

salt and pepper

To serve

100 g (3½ oz) baby spinach leaves

lemon wedges

Preparation time: 35 minutes, plus cooling
Cooking time: 30–40 minutes

1 Heat the oil in a saucepan, add the onion and cook gently for about 5 minutes or until softened. Add the rice and stir to coat all the grains with the oil. Stir in the vermouth and boil until it has almost all evaporated.

2 Add a ladleful of the hot stock and bubble gently, stirring frequently, until it has almost all been absorbed. Continue adding the stock, a ladleful at a time, allowing each to be almost all absorbed before adding the next, and stirring frequently. Total cooking time will be 15–20 minutes. The risotto is ready when the rice is tender but the grains are still firm, and the overall texture is moist and creamy.

3 Remove from the heat and season with salt and pepper to taste. Stir in the egg and Parmesan, then leave to cool completely.

4 Preheat the oven to 200°C (400°F, gas mark 6). Heat a lightly oiled ovenproof dish or baking tin in the oven. Mix the breadcrumbs with some seasoning on a large plate.

5 Spoon the risotto into 8 equal mounds on a large board. Press a cube of mozzarella into the centre of each mound, then press the risotto over the cheese so it is completely enclosed. With your hands, mould each mound into a neat egg-shaped croquette.

6 Roll the croquettes in the seasoned breadcrumbs until completely coated. Place in the hot ovenproof dish or tin and bake for 30–40 minutes, turning halfway through, until golden brown and crisp.

7 Make a heap of spinach leaves on 4 plates and top each one with 2 croquettes. Serve immediately, with lemon wedges to squeeze over.

Each serving provides ⓥ

kcal 352, **protein** 15 g, **fat** 11 g (of which saturated fat 4 g), **carbohydrate** 46 g (of which sugars 2 g), **fibre** 1 g

✓✓ A, B$_{12}$, calcium, zinc

✓ B$_1$, B$_2$, C, folate, niacin, copper, iron, potassium, selenium

Plus points

● Mozzarella cheese is lower in fat than many other cheese – Cheddar cheese has on average 34.4 g fat per 100 g (3½ oz), whereas the same weight of mozzarella cheese contains 21 g fat.

● Raw spinach is a good source of beta-carotene and provides vitamin C and E, all of which are antioxidants that help to protect against heart disease, strokes and cancer.

soups and starters

56

Some more ideas

● Stuff a small leaf of fresh basil or sage in the centre of each croquette with the mozzarella.

● Turn this into a lunch dish for 3 or 4 simply by serving the croquettes with a well-flavoured tomato or red pepper sauce spooned over, and a crisp salad alongside.

● Although mozzarella is the traditional cheese to use, cubes of creamy, blue-veined Dolcelatte, Brie, Camembert or taleggio cheeses could all be substituted.

● Make rice croquettes with chorizo. Cook the risotto as in the main recipe, but add 2 tbsp chopped fresh sage or 2 tsp dried sage instead of the Parmesan. Cut a 65 g chorizo sausage into 8 slices and fry in a dry pan for 5 minutes or until crisp. Drain well on kitchen paper. Stuff each croquette with a slice of chorizo instead of the mozzarella cubes. Serve the croquettes on a bed of rocket leaves and scatter over a few halved cherry tomatoes to garnish.

Quick Main Dishes

Sustaining suppers in 30 minutes or less

Use canned beans, rice and quick-cooking grains to make
fabulous fast meals. Sausage and beans are always
popular with the family, and here they come with a
potato and parsnip mash on top. Beans can also be used
to make tasty burgers, mixed with Cheddar cheese and
vegetables, or try creamy butter beans and bacon on thick
slices of toast. Favourite spicy rice dishes, such as pilaf,
kedgeree and jambalaya, only need
a salad on the side, while an
Oriental-style dish of wholewheat
grains, stir-fried vegetables and
tofu is a delicious meal in one pot.

Sausage and bean hotpot

For this family supper dish, grilled sausages in a spicy tomato and bean sauce are topped with a fluffy potato and parsnip mash. Use meaty pork sausages – there are many varieties available, with different flavours and seasonings, so you can ring the changes. Serve with a green vegetable such as steamed broccoli.

Serves 4

4 good-quality, high-meat-content pork
  sausages, about 280 g (10 oz) in total
1 can chopped tomatoes, about 400 g
2 cans red kidney or borlotti beans, about
  410 g each, drained and rinsed
2 tbsp tomato chutney
2 tsp paprika

Potato and parsnip topping

750 g (1 lb 10 oz) potatoes, peeled and cut
  into cubes
1 large parsnip, about 170 g (6 oz), chopped
2 tbsp semi-skimmed milk
1 tbsp extra virgin olive oil
salt and pepper

Preparation and cooking time: 30 minutes

1 Preheat the grill to moderate. Place the sausages under the grill and cook for about 15 minutes, turning regularly, until evenly browned all over and cooked through.

2 Meanwhile, cook the potatoes and parsnip in a saucepan of boiling water for 15 minutes or until tender.

3 At the same time, put the tomatoes with their juice, the kidney or borlotti beans, chutney and paprika in a saucepan and heat gently until bubbling.

4 Remove the sausages from the grill (leave the grill on). Allow to cool slightly, then cut each one diagonally into 4 thick slices. Add them to the tomato and bean mixture. Pour into a flameproof dish.

5 Drain the potatoes and parsnip, and mash with the milk and olive oil. Season with salt and pepper to taste.

6 Spoon the mash evenly over the top of the sausage and bean mixture. Brown under the grill for 5 minutes or until golden and crisp. Serve hot.

Another idea

● For sausage and lentil stew with couscous, grill 4 garlicky Italian pork sausages or Toulouse sausages (choose those with a high meat content). Meanwhile, pour 250 ml (8½ fl oz) boiling vegetable stock over 250 g (8½ oz) couscous and stir, then cover and leave for 5 minutes so the couscous can absorb the stock. Fluff up with a fork, then stir in the grated zest and juice of 1 lemon, 2 tbsp capers and 3 tbsp chopped fresh flat-leaf parsley. Cover and keep warm. Heat 1 can chopped tomatoes, about 400 g, with 1 can green lentils, about 410 g, drained and rinsed. Add 2 tbsp chopped fresh mint and seasoning to taste. Thickly slice each sausage into 4 and add to the tomato and lentil mixture. Spoon the sausages and sauce over the couscous. Garnish with sprigs of flat-leaf parsley and serve hot.

Plus points

● Including pulses in a dish such as this allows the quantity of meat to be reduced, while maintaining a good protein content. Using a mixture of pulses and meat also reduces the amount of fat in the dish.

● Canned tomatoes are an ideal item to keep in the storecupboard, not only because they are convenient, but also because they are very nutritious. Lycopene, a valuable antioxidant contained in tomatoes, is enhanced by cooking, so canned tomatoes are a better source than fresh tomatoes.

Each serving provides

kcal 525, protein 24 g, fat 18 g (of which saturated fat 5.5 g), carbohydrate 72 g (of which sugars 17 g), fibre 13 g

✓✓✓	B₁, B₆, C
✓✓	E, folate, niacin, calcium, copper, iron, potassium, zinc
✓	A, B₂, B₁₂, selenium

Basmati chicken pilaf

This colourful one-pot dish is very simple to make and ideal for a tasty and nutritious mid-week meal. Coconut milk, gentle spices and fresh coriander add an exotically fragrant note. Serve with a mixed green salad.

Serves 4

2 tbsp extra virgin olive oil

1 onion, chopped

1 garlic clove, crushed

1 red pepper, seeded and diced

340 g (12 oz) skinless boneless chicken breasts (fillets), cut into thin strips

170 g (6 oz) button mushrooms, halved

2 courgettes, sliced

300 g (10½ oz) basmati rice, rinsed

1 tsp ground coriander

1 tsp ground cumin

1 tsp ground cinnamon

150 ml (5 fl oz) coconut milk

400 ml (14 fl oz) hot chicken or vegetable stock

2 tbsp chopped fresh coriander

salt and pepper

sprigs of fresh coriander to garnish

Preparation time: 10 minutes, plus 5 minutes standing

Cooking time: 20–25 minutes

Each serving provides

kcal 459, **protein** 29 g, **fat** 8 g (of which saturated fat 1 g), **carbohydrate** 68 g (of which sugars 7 g), **fibre** 2 g

✓✓✓	A, C, niacin
✓✓	B₆, copper
✓	B₁, B₂, folate, iron, potassium, selenium, zinc

1 Heat the oil in a saucepan and add the onion, garlic, red pepper and chicken. Cook, stirring, over a fairly high heat for 4–5 minutes or until the chicken has lost its raw look.

2 Add the mushrooms, courgettes, rice, ground coriander, cumin and cinnamon. Cook, stirring, for 1 minute.

3 Pour in the coconut milk and hot stock, and season with salt and pepper to taste. Bring to the boil, then cover, reduce the heat and simmer for 10–15 minutes or until the rice is tender and has absorbed the liquid.

4 Remove from the heat. Stir in the chopped coriander, then cover again and leave to stand for 5 minutes. Serve hot, garnished with coriander sprigs.

Some more ideas

• Use chestnut or portabellini mushrooms instead of button mushrooms.

• Make a ginger turkey pilaf, using turkey breast steak instead of the chicken. Fry in the oil with 2 sliced leeks, 1 crushed garlic clove, a 2.5 cm (1 in) piece of fresh root ginger, finely chopped, and 1 seeded and finely chopped fresh red chilli. Add the basmati rice with 250 g (8½ oz) sliced baby corn and 170 g (6 oz) frozen peas. In step 3, replace the coconut milk with dry white wine or additional stock, then cook as in the main recipe. In step 4, stir in chopped fresh flat-leaf parsley instead of coriander plus 30 g (1 oz) butter, and leave to stand for 5 minutes before serving.

Plus points

• Basmati rice scores lower on the Glycaemic Index than any other variety of rice. This means that it is digested more slowly and so provides long-term energy.

• Chicken provides excellent amounts of protein as well as B vitamins, particularly niacin. Eaten without the skin, chicken is healthily low in fat.

• Mushrooms are a good source of copper, a mineral that is important for healthy bones. Copper also helps the body to absorb iron from food.

quick main dishes

Smoked trout kedgeree with quail's eggs

Smoked trout takes the place of the more traditional smoked haddock in this fragrant rice dish from the Raj, which was originally served for breakfast. This version makes the perfect quick supper, with poppadoms and mango chutney on the side, plus a tomato and cucumber salad.

Serves 4

300 g (10½ oz) long-grain white rice
1 litre (1¾ pints) vegetable stock or water
8 quail's eggs
1 tbsp extra virgin olive oil
1 large onion, finely chopped
1 fresh red chilli, seeded and sliced
1 tbsp korma curry paste
3 tbsp Greek-style yogurt
280 g (10 oz) smoked trout fillets, skinned and flaked into large pieces
4 tbsp chopped fresh coriander
55 g (2 oz) toasted flaked almonds
salt

Preparation and cooking time: 30 minutes

1 Put the rice in a pan, add the stock or water and bring to the boil. Stir, then cover and simmer very gently for 10–15 minutes or until the rice is tender and has absorbed all the liquid.

2 While the rice is cooking, put the quail's eggs in a small pan of water and bring to the boil. Remove from the heat and leave to stand for 30 seconds, then drain off the water. Cover with fresh cold water, and leave until cool enough to handle. Peel the eggs and cut each one in half.

3 Heat the oil in a large frying pan, add the onion and chilli, and cook, stirring frequently, for 10 minutes or until the onion is soft and has started to turn golden. Add the curry paste and cook, stirring, for 1 minute.

4 Tip the rice into the frying pan. Add the yogurt and toss together until well blended. Mix in the smoked trout, coriander and almonds. Place the quail's eggs on top and heat through briefly, then serve.

Another idea

● To make lemon-scented kipper kedgeree, use basmati rice instead of long-grain, and cook in water with 4 fresh bay leaves, rather than stock. Meanwhile, grill 2 large kippers, about 550 g (1¼ lb) in total, for 5 minutes; remove the skin and bones and flake the flesh. In step 3, omit the curry paste. In step 4, with the rice and yogurt stir in 2 generous pinches of saffron threads mixed with the grated zest and juice of 1 large lemon. Replace the almonds with coarsely chopped cashew nuts. Serve with lemon wedges to squeeze over.

Each serving provides

kcal 573, protein 28 g, fat 21 g (of which saturated fat 4 g), carbohydrate 73 g (of which sugars 6 g), fibre 2 g

✓✓✓	B_{12}, phosphorus
✓✓	B_6, E, niacin, copper, selenium, zinc
✓	A, B_1, B_2, calcium, iron, potassium

Plus points

● Rainbow trout is usually used to make smoked trout. Like other oily fish, it is a rich source of the heart-healthy omega-3 fatty acids. Trout also contains useful amounts of potassium and iodine.
● Nuts and Greek-style yogurt add extra protein to this well-balanced dish.

quick main dishes

64

Three-bean and ham stir-fry

If you've never before thought of using pulses in a stir-fry, here's a satisfying recipe to try. It combines 2 different kinds of canned beans with fresh green beans for contrast, plus strips of ham, onions and a creamy mustard sauce with a hint of lemon to add to the flavours. Tossed with pasta, this is a great meal made in one pot.

Serves 4

250 g (8½ oz) short-cut macaroni

170 g (6 oz) fine green beans, cut in half

2 tsp extra virgin olive oil

15 g (½ oz) unsalted butter

1 bunch large spring onions, about 300 g (10½ oz) in total, sliced

2 tbsp crème fraîche

2 tsp wholegrain mustard

grated zest of 1 lemon

225 g (8 oz) thickly sliced cooked ham or smoked pork loin, trimmed of all fat and cut into fine strips

1 can red kidney beans, about 410 g, drained and rinsed

1 can cannellini beans, about 410 g, drained and rinsed

3 tbsp chopped parsley

salt and pepper

Preparation and cooking time: 30 minutes

1 Cook the pasta in a large pan of boiling water for 10–12 minutes, or according to the packet instructions, until al dente. Add the green beans for the last 3 minutes of the cooking time. Drain well.

2 While the pasta is cooking, heat the oil and butter in a large non-stick frying pan or wok until the butter starts to sizzle. Add the spring onions and cook for 3–4 minutes over a moderate heat, turning frequently, until softened.

3 Blend together the crème fraîche, mustard and lemon zest, and add to the pan or wok. Stir in the ham or pork and the canned kidney and cannellini beans. Cook gently for 2–3 minutes, stirring frequently, until piping hot.

4 Season with salt and pepper to taste. Add the pasta and green beans, and stir to mix. Sprinkle over the parsley and serve.

Some more ideas

● For a vegetarian version, replace the ham or pork with a 225 g (8 oz) packet of smoked tofu, cut into 2.5 cm (1 in) cubes.

● Make a smoked turkey, apple and bean sauté. Core and thickly slice 2 dessert apples. Cook in 15 g (½ oz) butter in a non-stick frying pan over a moderate heat for 3–4 minutes, turning once, until golden on both sides and just tender. Remove and set aside. Put 1 can borlotti beans, about 410 g, and 1 can flageolet beans, about 410 g, both drained and rinsed, in the pan. Add 225 g (8 oz) thickly sliced smoked turkey, cut into fine strips, 3 tbsp apple juice and 2 tsp maple syrup. Heat through gently for 2 minutes, stirring occasionally, then return the apples to the pan together with 1 tbsp chopped fresh sage. Season to taste. Heat for a further minute. Serve with crusty French bread.

Plus points

● Pulses such as red kidney and cannellini beans have a low GI (Glycaemic Index) factor, which means they release energy slowly into the bloodstream and so can help to control hunger and appetite.

● Like all onions, spring onions contain some vitamin C and B vitamins.

● Green beans are a good source of dietary fibre and contain valuable amounts of folate.

Each serving provides

kcal 575, **protein** 30 g, **fat** 20 g (of which saturated fat 8 g), **carbohydrate** 73 g (of which sugars 10 g), **fibre** 12 g

✓✓ A, B₁,C, folate, niacin, copper, iron, potassium, selenium, zinc

✓ B₂, B₆, calcium

Cannellini bean burgers

These nutritious vegetarian burgers are tasty enough to appeal to everyone. They hold their shape well yet remain wonderfully moist when grilled. A cherry tomato and basil salad is the perfect complement.

Serves 4

5 tsp extra virgin olive oil

1 small onion, finely chopped

1 carrot, coarsely grated

2 tsp sun-dried tomato paste

2 cans cannellini beans, about 410 g each, drained and rinsed

55 g (2 oz) fresh white breadcrumbs (made by grating the bread)

55 g (2 oz) mature Cheddar cheese, grated

2 tbsp chopped parsley

4 large wholemeal baps

salt and pepper

frisée to garnish

Cherry tomato salad

1 tbsp extra virgin olive oil

1 tsp lemon juice

340 g (12 oz) cherry tomatoes, a mixture of red and yellow if possible, quartered

1 tbsp torn or shredded fresh basil

Preparation time: 20 minutes

Cooking time: 8–10 minutes

Each serving provides

kcal 500, **protein** 22 g, **fat** 15 g (of which saturated fat 5 g), **carbohydrate** 75 g (of which sugars 11 g), **fibre** 14 g

✓✓✓	A, selenium
✓✓	B₁, C, niacin, calcium, copper, iron, zinc
✓	B₂, B₆, E, folate, potassium

1 Heat 3 tsp of the oil in a non-stick frying pan, add the onion and cook for 5 minutes, stirring frequently, until softened. Add the grated carrot and cook for a further 2 minutes, stirring. Remove from the heat and stir in the tomato paste.

2 Preheat the grill to moderate. Tip the cannellini beans into a bowl and mash with a potato masher to break them up roughly. Add the cooked vegetables, breadcrumbs, cheese, parsley, and salt and pepper to taste.

3 Use your hands to mix all the ingredients together, then divide into 4 portions. Shape each into a large burger, about 10 cm (4 in) in diameter and 2.5 cm (1 in) thick.

4 Lightly brush the burgers on both sides with the remaining 2 tsp olive oil and place on the rack of the grill pan. Cook for 4–5 minutes on each side or until slightly crisp and hot all the way through.

5 Meanwhile, make the salad by whisking together the oil, lemon juice and seasoning to taste in a bowl. Add the tomatoes and basil.

6 Split the baps in half using a serrated knife. If liked, toast under the grill with the burgers for the last 2–3 minutes of cooking. Place the bean burgers inside and serve, with the tomato salad and a garnish of frisée.

Some more ideas

• For spicy bean burgers, replace the tomato paste with 1½ tsp of your favourite curry paste.

• Make soya bean and olive burgers. Cook a bunch of finely chopped spring onions and 1 seeded and finely chopped fresh red chilli in the 3 tsp oil for 3–4 minutes to soften, then stir in 1 grated courgette and cook for 2 more minutes; omit the tomato paste. Mash 2 cans soya beans, about 410 g each, drained and rinsed. Add the cooked vegetables together with 55 g (2 oz) chopped stoned black olives, a dash of soy sauce, 2 tbsp chopped fresh coriander and seasoning to taste. Shape into 8 burgers and brush with the remaining 2 tsp oil. Grill for 3–4 minutes on each side. Serve in halved pitta breads, allowing 2 burgers per person, and add 450 g (1 lb) plum tomatoes and ½ cucumber, both sliced.

Plus points

• Not only are cannellini beans packed with protein, they also contain many minerals, including iron, potassium, phosphorus and manganese.

• Cheese is a very nutritious food to include in the diet. In general, the harder, more dense cheeses such as Cheddar contain more protein, calcium, phosphorus and B vitamins than softer cheeses.

quick main dishes

Seafood jambalaya

Mixed with rice and plenty of vegetables, a small amount of succulent salmon and prawns goes a long way, making a good balance of protein and carbohydrate in this temptingly spicy, Louisiana-style dish. As an added bonus for the busy cook, it is cooked in just one pan and makes a complete meal on its own.

Serves 4

1½ tbsp extra virgin olive oil

1 onion, chopped

2 celery sticks, sliced

1 green or red pepper, seeded and cut into strips

2 garlic cloves, crushed

½ tsp ground ginger

½ tsp cayenne pepper

1 tsp mild chilli powder

340 g (12 oz) long-grain white rice

900 ml (1½ pints) hot vegetable stock

1 can chopped tomatoes, about 225 g

3 tbsp coarsely chopped parsley

100 g (3½ oz) peeled large raw prawns

200 g (7 oz) skinned salmon fillet, cut into 2.5 cm (1 in) cubes

dash of Tabasco sauce (optional)

salt and pepper

Preparation and cooking time: 30 minutes

Each serving provides

kcal 483, protein 22 g, fat 11 g (of which saturated fat 2 g), carbohydrate 80 g (of which sugars 5 g), fibre 2 g

✓✓✓	B$_{12}$, C
✓✓	B$_6$, E, niacin, copper, selenium, zinc
✓	B$_1$, folate, iron, potassium

1 Heat the oil in a large, wide pan over a moderately high heat. Add the onion and cook, stirring, for about 3 minutes. Add the celery, green or red pepper, garlic, ginger, cayenne, chilli powder and rice, and cook, stirring, for 2 minutes.

2 Pour in the hot stock and stir well, then reduce the heat so that the stock is simmering gently. Cover the pan with a tight-fitting lid and simmer for 15 minutes.

3 Stir in the chopped tomatoes with their juice and 2 tbsp of the parsley, then add the prawns and salmon. Cover again and simmer for 3–4 minutes or until the seafood is just cooked and the rice has absorbed most of the liquid and is tender.

4 Add the Tabasco sauce, if using, and salt and pepper to taste. Sprinkle with the remaining 1 tbsp parsley and serve hot.

Some more ideas

• Use brown rice instead of white. It will take 30–40 minutes to cook and will need about 150 ml (5 fl oz) more stock.

• For a pork and smoked sausage jambalaya, cut 200 g (7 oz) pork fillet (tenderloin) into thin strips and brown in 1 tbsp extra virgin olive oil, then remove from the pan and set aside. Add 1 chopped red onion to the pan and cook for

5 minutes or until almost soft. Stir in the rice and cook for 2–3 minutes, then pour in 750 ml (1¼ pints) vegetable stock. Cover and simmer for 10 minutes. Stir in 1 can tomatoes with added peppers and basil, about 400 g, with the juice, and 200 g (7 oz) sliced courgettes. Cover and cook for a further 5 minutes. Return the pork to the pan together with 115 g (4 oz) sliced smoked sausage and cook, covered, for 5 more minutes or until all the liquid has been absorbed and the rice is tender. Serve sprinkled with 2 tbsp chopped parsley.

Plus points

• Prawns are low in fat and high in protein. They are also a good source of the antioxidant mineral selenium, which helps to protect the cardiovascular system.

• Salmon provides vitamins B$_6$ and B$_{12}$ and the minerals selenium and potassium.

• Rice requires more water for growing than any other cereal crop. However, the main purpose of the standing water in paddy fields is to drown the 'weed' competition that the rice seedlings face.

Butter beans and bacon on toast

Here's a new version of beans on toast, combining creamy butter beans with crisp bacon, curd cheese and mustard. With a crisp salad alongside, it makes a super meal that is ready to serve in about 15 minutes.

Serves 4

15 g (½ oz) butter

4 rashers lean back bacon, rinded and
   chopped

1 bunch spring onions, sliced

85 g (3 oz) watercress, tough stalks removed,
   roughly chopped

2 cans butter beans, about 410 g each,
   drained and rinsed

55 g (2 oz) curd cheese

1 tsp Dijon mustard

8 thick slices of wholemeal bread

salt and pepper

Red leaf salad

2 tbsp extra virgin olive oil

2 tsp lemon juice

1 tsp clear honey

1 small head radicchio, cut into thin wedges

1 small Lollo Rosso lettuce, leaves separated

Preparation and cooking time: 15 minutes

1 For the salad, put the oil, lemon juice and honey in a salad bowl and add salt and pepper to taste. Whisk together. Add the radicchio and Lollo Rosso to the bowl and set aside (do not toss yet).

2 Preheat the grill. Melt the butter in a large non-stick frying pan until beginning to sizzle. Add the bacon and spring onions, and cook over a moderate heat for about 3 minutes, stirring frequently, until the bacon begins to colour and the onions are just tender.

3 Add the watercress and cook for a few seconds, stirring, then add the butter beans, curd cheese, mustard, and salt and pepper to taste. Lower the heat and cook for 2 minutes, stirring all the time, until the mixture is piping hot.

4 While the bean and bacon mixture is cooking, toast the slices of bread under the grill. Spoon the bean and bacon mixture onto the hot toast. Quickly toss the salad, and serve.

Some more ideas

• For vegetarians, you can leave out the bacon. Scatter 55 g (2 oz) chopped toasted walnuts over the salad, to replace the protein provided by the bacon.

• Make borlotti bean and blue cheese ciabatta. Put 2 cans borlotti beans, about 410 g each, drained and rinsed, in a saucepan with 85 g (3 oz) crumbled Gorgonzola cheese, 2 tbsp plain low-fat yogurt and 2 tbsp quark. Heat very gently, stirring frequently, until the cheese melts and the beans are hot. Stir in 1 tbsp red pesto and serve on ciabatta rolls, split in half and lightly toasted. Accompany with a fennel and rocket salad. For the dressing, whisk 2 tbsp extra virgin olive oil with 1 tsp balsamic vinegar, 2 tbsp orange juice and seasoning to taste. Add 1 thinly sliced fennel bulb, 85 g (3 oz) rocket leaves, 1 thinly sliced small red onion and 30 g (1 oz) stoned black olives, and toss just before serving with the ciabatta.

Plus points

• As their name suggests, butter beans have a buttery flavour when cooked. They offer plenty of dietary fibre, essential for a healthy digestive system.

• Trimmed of fat, lean back bacon is a high-protein, low-fat ingredient that provides particularly useful amounts of vitamin B_1, which is essential for maintaining a healthy nervous system.

• Watercress contains some powerful phytochemicals that appear to help protect the body against cancer.

Each serving provides

kcal 453, protein 23 g, fat 16 g (of which saturated fat 5 g), carbohydrate 58 g (of which sugars 7 g), fibre 11 g

✓✓✓	selenium
✓✓	A, B_1, C, niacin, copper, iron, zinc
✓	B_6, E, folate, calcium, potassium

quick main dishes

72

Spaghetti with chickpeas, spinach and spicy tomato sauce

Here's a colourful and easy vegetarian dish that makes a satisfying main course all on its own. It's a delicious way to mix pasta and beans, in this case chickpeas, for a good balance of protein and starchy carbohydrate.

Serves 4

2 tbsp extra virgin olive oil

1 onion, chopped

1 garlic clove, crushed

1 celery stick, finely chopped

1 can chopped tomatoes, about 400 g

340 g (12 oz) spaghetti

2 cans chickpeas, about 410 g each, drained and rinsed

½ tsp Tabasco sauce, or to taste

170 g (6 oz) baby spinach leaves

salt and pepper

55 g (2 oz) pecorino cheese, freshly grated

fresh flat-leaf parsley leaves to garnish

Preparation and cooking time: 20–25 minutes

Each serving provides Ⓥ

kcal 582, protein 27 g, fat 15 g (of which saturated fat 4 g), carbohydrate 89 g (of which sugars 9 g), fibre 10 g

✓✓✓	A
✓✓	C, E, folate, niacin, calcium, copper, iron, potassium, zinc
✓	B₁, B₆

1 Heat the olive oil in a heavy-based saucepan, add the onion and garlic, and cook over a moderate heat for 3–4 minutes, stirring occasionally, until softened.

2 Add the celery and fry, stirring, for 1–2 minutes, then stir in the chopped tomatoes with their juice and bring to the boil. Reduce the heat and simmer gently, stirring occasionally, for about 15 minutes or until thick.

3 Meanwhile, cook the spaghetti in a large pan of boiling water for 10–12 minutes, or according to the packet instructions, until al dente.

4 When the sauce is cooked, stir in the chickpeas and Tabasco sauce. Add the spinach leaves and simmer for 1–2 minutes, stirring, until the spinach wilts. Season with salt and pepper to taste.

5 Drain the spaghetti and toss with the chickpeas and tomato sauce. Scatter over the parsley leaves, and serve immediately, sprinkled with the pecorino cheese.

Some more ideas

● For tagliatelle with cannellini beans, use tagliatelle or fettuccine instead of spaghetti, and replace the chickpeas with canned cannellini or haricot beans. Instead of spinach, add 200 g (7 oz) cooked asparagus spears, cut into 2.5 cm (1 in) lengths, to the sauce. Just before serving, stir in 85 g (3 oz) thin strips of trimmed Parma ham; omit the pecorino cheese.

● Grill 4 lean rashers of back bacon until crisp and golden, then drain well and chop roughly. Stir into the tomato sauce with the chickpeas. Reduce the pecorino cheese to 30 g (1 oz).

Plus points

● Despite its name, the chickpea is not really a pea but a seed. Chickpeas contain good amounts of iron, manganese and folate, and are richer in vitamin E than most other pulses.

● Pasta, like bread and potatoes, has a reputation for being fattening, but in fact it is healthily low in fat – it's butter, cheese and rich sauces that pile on the calories and fat.

● By cooking the spinach leaves in the sauce very briefly, just to wilt them, all their juices and the maximum nutrients are retained.

quick main dishes

Wholewheat and vegetable pan-fry with teriyaki tofu

Here pre-cooked wholewheat grains are cooked in stock, then tossed with **fresh ginger and Oriental vegetables** to make the perfect partner for Japanese-style marinated tofu. **This is a delicious, nutritious dish made in minutes.**

Serves 4

600 ml (1 pint) vegetable stock

200 g (7 oz) pre-cooked wholewheat grains

2 garlic cloves, crushed

1 tbsp finely grated fresh root ginger

2 tbsp dark soy sauce

1 tbsp mirin

1 tbsp sunflower oil

1 tbsp clear honey

1 tsp Chinese five-spice powder

1 packet tofu, about 285 g, cut into bite-sized triangles

Vegetable pan-fry

2 tbsp sunflower oil

2 garlic cloves, crushed

1 tbsp finely grated fresh root ginger

1 large red pepper, seeded and cut into long matchsticks

1 leek, cut into long matchsticks

250 g (8½ oz) bean sprouts

Preparation and cooking time: 30 minutes

Each serving provides

kcal 375, **protein** 16 g, **fat** 13 g (of which saturated fat 2 g), **carbohydrate** 50 g (of which sugars 12 g), **fibre** 6 g

✓✓✓	A, C, E, calcium, copper
✓✓	B₁, niacin, iron
✓	B₆, folate, potassium, zinc

1 Pour the vegetable stock into a saucepan and bring to the boil. Add the wholewheat grains and simmer for 15–20 minutes or until they are tender and the stock has been absorbed.

2 Meanwhile, for the teriyaki tofu, mix together the garlic, ginger, soy sauce, mirin, sunflower oil, honey and five-spice powder in a bowl. Add the tofu and turn until all the pieces are coated in the mixture. Set aside to marinate while cooking the vegetables.

3 Heat the oil in a wok or large frying pan, add the garlic and ginger, and stir-fry for a few seconds. Add the red pepper and leek strips, and stir-fry for 3–4 minutes or until softened. Stir in the bean sprouts and stir-fry for 3 minutes.

4 Add the wholewheat grains to the wok. Hold a sieve over the wok and tip the tofu mixture into it, straining the marinade into the wok. Toss until the wholewheat grains and marinade are mixed with the vegetables. Gently toss in the tofu and cook for 1–2 minutes longer or until heated through. Serve immediately.

Another idea

● To make a Mediterranean wholewheat and vegetable pan-fry, mix together 2 crushed garlic cloves, 8 finely chopped sun-dried tomatoes packed in oil, drained, 1 tbsp oil from the jar of tomatoes, and 10 shredded fresh basil leaves from a 15 g packet (reserve the rest). Add the tofu and set aside to marinate. In step 3, omit the ginger, leek and bean sprouts, and stir-fry 1 thinly sliced large onion and 2 courgettes, cut into strips, with the red pepper and garlic. Add the wholewheat grains, 55 g (2 oz) black olives, the remaining shredded basil, and the tofu and tomato mixture. Heat through, stirring and tossing, and serve.

Plus points

● Wholewheat grains are low in fat and high in starchy carbohydrate. Because the whole of the grain is eaten, they are also a good source of dietary fibre.

● Evidence is beginning to suggest that including soya beans and products made from soya beans, such as tofu, in the diet regularly may help to reduce the risk of certain cancers and heart disease

● Bean sprouts, like other sprouted seeds, are rich in B vitamins and vitamin C.

Oat-crusted mackerel fillets with orange and mustard

The crisp coating on these fillets seals in all the flavour of the fish, as well as adding texture and beneficial fibre. They can be served with baked or boiled potatoes or bread, plus a salad or seasonal vegetables.

Serves 4

2 oranges

140 g (5 oz) medium oatmeal

2 tsp Dijon mustard

8 small mackerel fillets, about 75 g (2½ oz) each

2 egg whites, lightly beaten with a fork

2 tbsp extra virgin olive oil

salt and pepper

Preparation time: 15 minutes

Cooking time: about 15 minutes

1 Preheat the oven to 220°C (425°F, gas mark 7). Finely grate the zest from one of the oranges. Cut away all the peel and white pith from both the oranges, then cut out the segments from the surrounding membrane. Set the orange segments aside.

2 Mix together the oatmeal, mustard, orange zest, and salt and pepper to taste on a plate, stirring to incorporate the mustard evenly.

3 Brush each mackerel fillet with egg white, then press into the oatmeal mixture to coat thoroughly on both sides. Place on a lightly greased baking sheet and drizzle with the olive oil.

4 Bake for about 15 minutes, depending on the thickness of the fish, until it flakes easily when tested with a fork. Serve hot, topped with the orange segments.

Some more ideas

● Instead of orange segments, serve the mackerel with a tomato orange salsa. Dice the orange flesh and mix with 1 diced beef tomato, a little chopped red onion, and chopped fresh mint, crushed garlic and seasoning to taste.

● For herrings with a zesty oat crust, mix together 55 g (2 oz) rolled oats, 1 tbsp finely chopped fresh sage, 1 tsp grated or creamed horseradish, the grated zest of 1 lemon, and salt and pepper to taste. Tuck sprigs of fresh sage into the cavities of 4 whole boned herrings. Brush the fish with egg white and coat all over with the oat mixture. Drizzle with 1 tbsp extra virgin olive oil, and bake as in the main recipe for 15 minutes.

Plus points

● Oatmeal is a good source of soluble fibre, which can help to reduce high blood cholesterol levels.

● Mackerel, like other oily fish, is an excellent source of vitamin D. Most people obtain their required amount of this vitamin from the action of sunlight on the skin. Those who are housebound, or remain indoors a lot, would benefit from including oily fish such as mackerel in their diet on a regular basis.

Each serving provides

kcal 559, **protein** 35 g, **fat** 33 g (of which saturated fat 6 g), **carbohydrate** 33 g (of which sugars 7 g), **fibre** 4 g

✓✓✓	B_{12}, C, niacin, selenium
✓✓	B_1, B_2, B_6, zinc
✓	A, E, folate, copper, iron, potassium

For Maximum Vitality

Salads with vitamin-rich fruit and vegetables

Combine cereal grains and pulses with raw fruit and vegetables to make dishes that are packed with flavour and texture, and wonderfully nutritious. Try nutty bulghur wheat tossed with baby corn and prawns in a spicy dressing, or kasha – toasted buckwheat – with seafood and sugarsnap peas. Pearl barley makes a tempting dish with black-eyed beans, spinach and tomatoes. Couscous and flageolet beans combine in a niçoise-style salad, perfect for a summer lunch. For a salad on the side, try a fruity rice mixture in a sensational tofu dressing.

Sweetcorn and wholewheat salad

Grains of wholewheat have a distinctive sweet, nutty flavour and slightly chewy texture. Here they are mixed with grilled fresh sweetcorn, toasted walnuts and crisp vegetables in a fragrant orange dressing to make a nutritious salad that is substantial enough to serve as a well-balanced main course.

Serves 4

300 g (10½ oz) pre-cooked wholewheat grains

1 bay leaf

2 corn on the cob

½ tbsp sunflower oil

75 g (2½ oz) walnuts, broken

1 red pepper, seeded and diced

115 g (4 oz) button mushrooms, sliced

½ cucumber, cut into small chunks

1 tbsp chopped fresh mint

1 egg, hard-boiled and sliced

salt and pepper

sprigs of fresh mint to garnish

Walnut and orange dressing

1 tsp Dijon mustard

½ tsp finely grated orange zest

1 tbsp orange juice

1 tbsp sunflower oil

1 tbsp walnut oil

Preparation and cooking time: 35 minutes, plus cooling

Each serving provides Ⓥ

kcal 559, **protein** 17 g, **fat** 24 g (of which saturated fat 3 g), **carbohydrate** 70 g (of which sugars 7 g), **fibre** 7 g

✓✓✓	A, C, copper
✓✓	B₁, E, niacin, iron
✓	B₂, B₆, folate, calcium, potassium, selenium, zinc

1 Put 900 ml (1½ pints) water in a saucepan and bring to the boil. Add the wholewheat grains and the bay leaf. Simmer for 15–20 minutes or until the wholewheat is tender and all the liquid has been absorbed. Discard the bay leaf and tip the wholewheat grains into a mixing bowl.

2 While the wholewheat grains are cooking, preheat the grill to moderately high. Brush the corn cobs all over with the sunflower oil, then put them on the rack of the grill pan. Grill for about 10 minutes, turning frequently, until tender and lightly charred in places. Set aside to cool slightly.

3 Meanwhile, spread out the walnuts in a baking tin. Put them under the grill and cook for 2–3 minutes or until lightly toasted, turning them frequently and watching them all the time as they burn easily. Set aside.

4 When the corn is cool enough to handle, cut the kernels off the cobs with a sharp knife. Add them to the wholewheat grains.

5 To make the dressing, whisk together the mustard, orange zest and juice, sunflower oil and walnut oil. Season with salt and pepper to taste. Drizzle the dressing over the warm wholewheat grains and corn, and toss well to mix. Leave to cool completely.

6 Add the red pepper, mushrooms, cucumber, mint and toasted walnuts to the wholewheat mixture and toss gently together. Taste and add more seasoning, if needed. Serve at room temperature, garnished with slices of hard-boiled egg and sprigs of mint.

Plus points

• Wholewheat grains are an excellent source of B vitamins and vitamin E. They are also a useful source of the essential minerals iron, selenium and zinc.

• Polyunsaturated oils, such as sunflower oil, contain large amounts of vitamin E, which prevents the oil from going rancid or 'off'. In the body, vitamin E helps to protect cell membranes from damage by free radicals.

• Walnuts provide useful amounts of vitamin E, many of the B vitamins and potassium.

for maximum vitality

Some more ideas

- If you cannot get pre-cooked wholewheat grains, soak ordinary wheat grains in cold water for 3–4 hours or overnight. The next day, drain and rinse, then put in a saucepan with 1.4 litres (2½ pints) cold water. Bring to the boil and simmer for 1½ hours or until tender and the water has been absorbed, stirring occasionally.
- For a barley and egg salad, heat 2 tsp sunflower oil in a large saucepan, add 300 g

(10½ oz) pearl barley and 1 crushed garlic clove, and cook gently for about 1 minute. Add a bay leaf and pour in 1.2 litres (2 pints) boiling vegetable stock. Bring to the boil, then reduce the heat and simmer for 35–40 minutes or until the barley is tender. Drain off any excess stock, then tip the barley into a bowl and leave to cool. Mix in 170 g (6 oz) tiny broccoli florets, 170 g (6 oz) tiny cauliflower florets, 1 seeded and sliced yellow pepper and a bunch of sliced

spring onions. For the dressing, whisk together 2 tbsp sunflower oil, 1 tsp toasted sesame oil, 2 tsp sherry vinegar, 2 tsp light soy sauce, the juice squeezed from a 2.5 cm (1 in) piece of grated fresh root ginger, and pepper to taste. Drizzle over the salad. Add 55 g (2 oz) toasted sunflower seeds and 15 g (½ oz) toasted sesame seeds and toss together. Gently mix in 4 hard-boiled eggs, cut into wedges, just before serving at room temperature.

Russian bean salad

Beetroot, soya beans and potatoes are tossed in a piquant soured cream dressing, then served on a salad of rocket, fennel and tomatoes in this delicious and refreshing main-course salad, which is suitable for vegetarians. Serve with dark rye bread so you can mop up all the creamy dressing.

Serves 4

150 g (5½ oz) dried soya beans, soaked overnight

450 g (1 lb) small new potatoes, scrubbed and halved

2 large shallots, thinly sliced

250 g (8½ oz) peeled, cooked beetroot (not pickled), diced

500 g (1 lb 2 oz) tomatoes, sliced

1 bulb of fennel, thinly sliced

55 g (2 oz) rocket

salt and pepper

Soured cream dressing

150 ml (5 fl oz) soured cream

150 g (5½ oz) plain low-fat yogurt

4 sweet and sour gherkins, finely chopped

2 tbsp creamed horseradish

1 tsp caster sugar

Preparation and cooking time: 3¼ hours, plus cooling

Each serving provides

kcal 386, protein 21 g, fat 16 g (of which saturated fat 6 g), carbohydrate 41 g (of which sugars 20 g), fibre 11 g

✓✓✓	C, folate, copper, potassium
✓✓	A, B₁, B₆, E, calcium, iron, selenium, zinc
✓	B₂, niacin

1 Drain the soaked beans and rinse under cold running water. Put in a saucepan and cover with fresh water. Bring to the boil and boil rapidly for 10–15 minutes, then partly cover and simmer for about 2½ hours or until tender. Drain and leave to cool.

2 Put the potatoes in a saucepan of boiling water and simmer for about 15 minutes or until just tender. Drain and leave until cool enough to handle.

3 Meanwhile, for the dressing, mix together the soured cream and yogurt in a large mixing bowl. Stir in the chopped gherkins, horseradish, sugar, and salt and pepper to taste.

4 Add the soya beans and shallots to the bowl and stir into the dressing. Cut the warm potatoes into cubes and add to the bean mixture, then gently fold in the beetroot.

5 Divide the tomatoes, fennel and rocket among 4 serving plates. Spoon the soya bean salad on top and serve immediately.

Another idea

• To make a broad bean and smoked haddock salad, substitute 2 cans broad beans, about 410 g each, drained and rinsed, for the soya beans. Instead of diced potatoes use small new potatoes and leave them whole. In the dressing, replace the horseradish with 2 tbsp chopped fresh dill. In step 4, omit the beetroot and add 225 g (8 oz) flaked cooked smoked haddock. Serve spooned onto a salad made by tossing together 1 seeded and thinly sliced red pepper, the segments from 2 large oranges, 45 g (1½ oz) watercress sprigs and 200 g (7 oz) torn romaine lettuce leaves.

Plus points

• Soya beans are rich in phytoestrogens and it is thought that they can help to protect against osteoporosis or brittle bone disease. Eating soya products also seems to help relieve many of the symptoms associated with the menopause.

• Traditionally, beetroot was believed to help keep blood healthy, probably because of its deep red colour. Indeed it does contain folate, a B vitamin that is needed for the prevention of anaemia.

• Fennel provides useful amounts of potassium and folate. In natural medicine it is believed to aid digestion, and to relieve wind and stomach cramps.

for maximum vitality

Couscous and flageolet niçoise

This is a bright, cheery salad with a real Mediterranean feel and flavour. Couscous is mixed with pale green flageolet beans, then tossed with fresh green beans, tomatoes and cucumber in a piquant dressing made with sun-dried tomatoes. Serve as a main course for a delightful summer lunch.

Serves 4

250 g (8½ oz) couscous

400 ml (14 fl oz) boiling water

1 tbsp extra virgin olive oil

1 tsp dried herbes de Provence

140 g (5 oz) green beans

½ cucumber

2 cans flageolet beans, about 410 g each, drained and rinsed

1 small red onion, finely chopped

200 g (7 oz) cherry tomatoes, cut in half

2 hard-boiled eggs, cut into quarters

8 anchovy fillets, drained and halved lengthways

75 g (2½ oz) black olives

Sun-dried tomato dressing

juice of 1 large lemon

2 tbsp extra virgin olive oil

1 tbsp finely chopped sun-dried tomatoes packed in oil

salt and pepper

Preparation time: 30 minutes

Each serving provides

kcal 424, **protein** 16 g, **fat** 18 g (of which saturated fat 3 g), **carbohydrate** 51 g (of which sugars 7 g), **fibre** 7 g

✓✓   B₁, B₁₂, C, E, iron

✓   A, B₂, B₆, folate, niacin, calcium, copper, potassium, selenium, zinc

1 First make the dressing. Combine the lemon juice, oil, sun-dried tomatoes and pepper to taste in a screwtop jar, cover and shake well to mix. Set aside.

2 Put the couscous into a large mixing bowl and pour over the boiling water. Stir in the olive oil and dried herbs, then cover and leave for 5 minutes or until the couscous has absorbed all the water. Uncover, stir to separate the grains and leave to cool.

3 Meanwhile, steam the green beans for 3–4 minutes or until tender but still crisp. Drain, then refresh under cold running water. Cut in half.

4 Cut the cucumber into thick slices, then cut each slice into 4 wedges. Stir the cucumber into the couscous, together with the flageolet beans, green beans, onion and tomatoes. Add the dressing and toss gently until well mixed. Taste and add salt and pepper, if necessary (remember that the anchovies and olives will be salty).

5 Transfer the salad to a serving bowl. Garnish with the hard-boiled egg quarters, anchovies and black olives, and serve.

Some more ideas

• For a vegetarian dish, simply omit the anchovies.

• Make a butter bean couscous salad, using 2 cans butter beans, about 410 g each, drained and rinsed, instead of flageolet beans. Replace the green beans with 2 large peppers, 1 red and 1 green, seeded and cut into thin strips. Make the dressing with 1 tbsp pesto, the juice of 1 lemon and 1 tbsp extra virgin olive oil. To garnish, instead of eggs, anchovies and olives, grill 100 g (3½ oz) lean back bacon, then drain well and crumble it over the salad.

Plus points

• Couscous, made from semolina, is the staple food in many North African countries. Like other cereals, it is low in fat and high in starchy carbohydrate.

• The vitamin C content in tomatoes is concentrated in the jelly-like substance surrounding the seeds.

• Anchovies offer calcium and phosphorus, both essential minerals for the maintenance of healthy bones and teeth. These minerals are retained in canned anchovies.

for maximum vitality

Bulghur wheat and prawn salad

Bulghur is coarsely ground wheat grains that have been parboiled, so it's quick and easy to prepare and makes an ideal storecupboard standby to use in salads as well as in hot dishes. This nutty-textured, colourful salad makes a great main dish for a summer lunch or picnic, and looks pretty enough for a special buffet.

Serves 4

250 g (8½ oz) bulghur wheat
1 small red onion, very thinly sliced
1 carrot, coarsely grated
1 tomato, diced
6 baby corn, sliced into rounds
½ cucumber, diced
200 g (7 oz) peeled cooked prawns
Lime and chilli dressing
4 tbsp extra virgin olive oil
2 tbsp lime juice
1 garlic clove, crushed
¼ tsp crushed dried chillies
salt and pepper

Preparation and cooking time: 20–25 minutes

1 Put the bulghur wheat in a saucepan and pour over 650 ml (22 fl oz) water. Bring to the boil, then simmer for 10 minutes or until the bulghur is tender and all the water has been absorbed. Tip the bulghur into a flat dish, spread out and allow to cool slightly.

2 Combine the onion, carrot, tomato, corn, cucumber and prawns in a large salad bowl. Add the bulghur wheat and stir together.

3 For the dressing, put the oil, lime juice, garlic, chilli flakes, and salt and pepper to taste in a small bowl. Whisk with a fork until combined. Stir the dressing into the salad, tossing to coat all the ingredients evenly. If not serving the salad immediately, cover and keep in the fridge.

Some more ideas

● For a bulghur wheat and feta salad, replace the prawns with 200 g (7 oz) diced feta cheese. Another alternative to the prawns is diced tofu.

● To make a bulghur wheat and ham salad, combine the cooked bulghur wheat with 150 g (5½ oz) thinly sliced Parma or Serrano ham, trimmed of all fat and cut into strips, 3 chopped spring onions, 1 seeded and diced yellow pepper, 200 g (7 oz) halved cherry tomatoes and 3 tbsp capers. Make the dressing by whisking together 4 tbsp extra virgin olive oil, 2 tbsp red wine vinegar, 1 tsp clear honey and 6 finely crushed allspice berries. Season to taste and toss with the salad.

Plus points

● Bulghur wheat is a good source of starchy carbohydrate, dietary fibre and B vitamins, as it contains all the particularly nutritious outer layers of the grain except the bran itself.

● The inclusion of raw vegetables in this salad not only adds texture and colour but also vitamins, particularly those with antioxidant properties.

● Prawns, like all seafish, contain iodine, which is needed for the formation of the thyroid hormones and the functioning of the thyroid gland itself.

Each serving provides

kcal 399, **protein** 19 g, **fat** 13 g (of which saturated fat 2 g), **carbohydrate** 53 g (of which sugars 5 g), **fibre** 2 g

✓✓✓	B_{12}
✓✓	A, niacin, copper, iron
✓	B_1, C, E, calcium, potassium, selenium, zinc

Tropical beef and rice salad

Ginger, honey, orange and chilli add exciting flavours to this colourful main course salad. It is perfect for a relaxed lunch as it can be mostly prepared ahead. Just before serving, add the fragrant papaya and baby salad leaves and sprinkle with toasted sesame seeds for the finishing touch.

Serves 4

340 g (12 oz) fillet steak, trimmed of all fat
    and cut into slices about 2 cm (¾ in) thick
280 g (10 oz) mixed basmati and wild rice
1 ripe papaya, peeled, seeded and sliced
6 spring onions, sliced on the diagonal
55 g (2 oz) mixed baby salad leaves, such as
    Lollo Rosso, cos and red chard
1 tbsp sesame seeds, toasted
salt and pepper

Marinade

3 tbsp sherry vinegar
2 tsp sunflower oil
1 large garlic clove, crushed
1 tsp finely chopped fresh root ginger
grated zest of 1 orange
1 tsp soft light brown sugar

Chilli and ginger dressing

3 tbsp sunflower oil
2 tbsp orange juice
2 tsp red wine vinegar
1 tsp clear honey
1 tsp finely chopped fresh root ginger
1 large fresh red chilli, seeded and finely
    chopped

Preparation and cooking time: about 45 minutes

1 Put all the ingredients for the marinade in a large shallow dish. Add salt and pepper to taste and mix well. Place the steak in the marinade, then cover and chill for 30 minutes, turning the slices over after 15 minutes so that both sides absorb the flavours.

2 Meanwhile, put the rice in a pan, add 750 ml (1¼ pints) water and bring to the boil. Cover and simmer very gently for about 20 minutes or until the rice is tender and has absorbed all the water. Remove from the heat.

3 While the rice is cooking, put all the ingredients for the dressing in a large salad bowl and whisk to combine. Season to taste. When the rice is cooked, tip it into the bowl and stir gently to mix with the dressing.

4 Preheat the grill to moderate. Remove the steak slices from the marinade and place on the rack of the grill pan. Grill for 5–6 minutes or until cooked to your taste, turning over halfway through cooking and brushing with any remaining marinade. Transfer the steak to a board and cut the slices across the grain into narrow strips. Add to the rice. (Cool and chill, if liked.)

5 Just before serving, add the papaya, spring onions and salad leaves, and toss gently together. Sprinkle with the sesame seeds and serve.

Plus points

● Wild rice is not true rice but the seeds of a North American wild aquatic grass. It contains more protein than other varieties of rice.

● Papaya is a useful source of vitamin A, present in the fruit as beta-carotene. This vitamin is needed to maintain good vision and plays a vital role in preventing blindness in many parts of the world where the diet would otherwise be deficient in vitamin A.

● Beef is considerably leaner than it used to be and well-trimmed lean cuts such as fillet steak can contain as little as 4.1% fat.

Each serving provides
kcal 513, **protein** 25 g, **fat** 16 g (of which saturated fat 3 g), **carbohydrate** 66 g (of which sugars 9 g), **fibre** 2 g

✓✓✓	C
✓✓	E
✓	A, copper, iron

Another idea

● For a lamb and asparagus salad with walnut rice, cut 340 g (12 oz) lamb neck fillet in half lengthways and trim off excess fat. Marinate in 2 tbsp red wine vinegar, 2 tsp sunflower oil, 1 tbsp orange juice, 1 crushed garlic clove and seasoning to taste for 30 minutes. Steam 125 g (4½ oz) asparagus tips for 7–8 minutes or until just tender, then cut in half. Make the dressing with 2 tbsp walnut oil, 1 tbsp sunflower oil, 2 tsp balsamic vinegar, 2 tbsp orange juice, the grated zest of 1 orange, 2 tbsp chopped fresh mint, a pinch of sugar and seasoning to taste. Toss the cooked rice with the dressing. Add the asparagus together with 1 small pineapple, peeled and chopped (about 280 g/10 oz flesh). Grill the lamb for about 10 minutes or until cooked through, then cut across into thin slices and add to the salad. Stir in 2 more tbsp chopped fresh mint and scatter over 55 g (2 oz) chopped toasted walnuts.

Warm kasha and seafood salad

Kasha, or toasted buckwheat grains, is an unusual base for a main dish salad and makes a pleasant change from rice and pasta. By including plenty of fresh raw vegetables, such as sugarsnap peas, cucumber, fennel and radishes, you add not only colour and flavour but valuable nutrients, too.

Serves 4

250 g (8½ oz) kasha (toasted buckwheat)

600 ml (1 pint) vegetable stock

3 tbsp sunflower oil

1 packet frozen mixed seafood, about 400 g, thawed

1 cucumber, diced

200 g (7 oz) sugarsnap peas, sliced

1 bulb of fennel, about 250 g (8½ oz), halved and thinly sliced

115 g (4 oz) radishes, thinly sliced

1 sheet nori seaweed to garnish

Fresh herb dressing

2 tbsp extra virgin olive oil

1 tbsp white wine vinegar

1 tsp Dijon mustard

2 tbsp chopped fresh mixed herbs

salt and pepper

Preparation and cooking time: 1½ hours

Each serving provides

kcal 514, protein 30 g, fat 18 g (of which saturated fat 2 g), carbohydrate 62 g (of which sugars 8 g), fibre 6.5 g

✓✓✓	B₁₂, copper, selenium, zinc
✓✓	B₁, B₆, C, E, niacin, iron, potassium
✓	A, B₂, folate, calcium

1 Put the kasha in a non-stick saucepan, pour over the stock and bring to the boil. Cover and simmer for about 5 minutes or until the kasha has absorbed all the stock.

2 Stir in 2 tbsp of the oil, cover and cook for 10 minutes. Then remove the lid and fork up the kasha, tossing and turning to separate the grains. Cook over a very low heat, uncovered, for a further 1 hour, tossing the kasha with a fork every 10 minutes to separate the grains.

3 Meanwhile, make the dressing. Put all the ingredients in a bowl and whisk together until thoroughly mixed.

4 Heat the remaining 1 tbsp oil in a wok or large frying pan. Add the seafood and stir-fry over a moderate heat for 2–3 minutes or until hot. Add the hot seafood to the kasha together with the cucumber, sugarsnap peas, fennel and radishes. Drizzle over the dressing and toss gently to mix.

5 Toast the sheet of seaweed by passing it over the flame of a gas burner, once on each side of the sheet, until it darkens and becomes crisp. Snip into fine strips with scissors, sprinkle over the salad and serve immediately.

Some more ideas

● Use mange-tout in place of sugarsnap peas.

● Instead of mixed seafood, use 400 g (14 oz) skinless boneless chicken or turkey breast, or lean beef or lamb steak, cut into thin strips. Stir-fry until cooked and lightly browned, then toss with the dressed kasha and vegetables.

● For a kasha and ham salad, replace the seafood with 250 g (8½ oz) lean cooked ham, cut into strips. Make a soy-based dressing by whisking together 4 tbsp extra virgin olive oil, 1 tbsp cider vinegar, 2 tsp light soy sauce, 2 tsp clear honey, 1 tsp wholegrain mustard and seasoning to taste. Instead of sugarsnap peas, fennel and radishes, add 2 finely chopped carrots, 170 g (6 oz) shredded Chinese leaves and 1–2 finely chopped or coarsely grated courgettes with the cucumber. Finish the salad with a sprinkling of 3–4 tbsp sunflower seeds rather than nori seaweed.

Plus points

● Buckwheat, native to central Asia, was introduced into Europe towards the end of the Middle Ages. It contains useful amounts of vitamin A and some of the B vitamins.

● Sugarsnap peas are a good source of vitamin C and they contain more dietary fibre than ordinary peas. This is because the edible pod contributes to the fibre content.

Minted barley and beans

The mild, sweet flavour and chewy texture of pearl barley is combined here with black-eyed beans and lots of colourful vegetables. A fresh-tasting tomato and mint dressing adds a summery feel to this wholesome salad. Serve on its own for lunch or supper, with some fresh fruit to follow.

Serves 4

1.4 litres (2½ pints) vegetable stock
strip of lemon zest
1 bay leaf
225 g (8 oz) baby leeks
1 tsp sunflower oil
225 g (8 oz) pearl barley
1 can black-eyed beans, about 410 g, drained
   and rinsed
6 firm, ripe plum tomatoes, about 500 g
   (1 lb 2 oz) in total, cut into thin wedges
140 g (5 oz) baby spinach leaves, shredded
1 bunch spring onions, about 85 g (3 oz),
   halved lengthways and shredded
sprig of fresh mint to garnish

Tomato and mint dressing

2 sun-dried tomatoes packed in oil, drained
   and finely chopped
2 tbsp oil from the sun-dried tomatoes
1 tbsp red wine vinegar
1 garlic clove, crushed
2 tbsp chopped fresh mint
1 tbsp chopped fresh chervil
salt and pepper

Preparation and cooking time: 1½ hours

1 Put the stock in a saucepan with the lemon zest and bay leaf. Bring to a rapid boil, then add the leeks and cook for 2–3 minutes or until just tender. Remove with a draining spoon and refresh briefly in cold water. Cut on the diagonal into 2.5 cm (1 in) lengths. Set aside.

2 Add the sunflower oil to the stock in the pan and bring back to the boil. Add the pearl barley, then cover and simmer for 30–40 minutes or until tender.

3 Spoon out 2 tbsp of the stock and reserve, then drain the barley. Discard the lemon zest and bay leaf. Tip the barley into a bowl and leave to cool.

4 Add the leeks, black-eyed beans, plum tomatoes, spinach and spring onions to the barley and stir gently to mix together.

5 To make the dressing, put the sun-dried tomatoes, oil, vinegar, garlic, mint, chervil, reserved stock, and salt and pepper to taste into a screwtop jar. Shake well until combined.

6 Drizzle the dressing over the barley and vegetables and toss to coat thoroughly. Serve at room temperature, garnished with a sprig of fresh mint.

Plus points

● Barley is believed to be the world's oldest cultivated grain. It is low in fat and rich in starchy carbohydrate, and, like other cereals, it is a good source of B vitamins.
● Although highly refined, weight for weight pearl barley provides more dietary fibre than brown rice.
● Spinach contains oxalic acid, which binds with iron, making most of it unavailable to the body. Eating spinach with something that is a good source of vitamin C, such as tomatoes, can increase iron uptake.

Each serving provides ⓥ

kcal 476, **protein** 14 g, **fat** 19 g (of which saturated fat 3 g), **carbohydrate** 67 g (of which sugars 7 g), **fibre** 6 g

✓✓✓	A, C, E, folate, copper
✓✓	B₁, B₆, iron, potassium, zinc
✓	niacin, calcium

for maximum vitality

Some more ideas

● Make a dilled barley and smoked salmon salad using 170 g (6 oz) smoked salmon, cut into strips, instead of the black-eyed beans. Replace the leeks with fine asparagus spears, preparing them in the same way. Add to the cooked barley together with the smoked salmon, spring onions, 1 halved and very thinly sliced bulb of fennel and 225 g (8 oz) halved red and yellow cherry tomatoes. For the dressing, whisk 2 tbsp sunflower oil with 2 tsp lemon juice, ½ tsp Dijon mustard, 3 tbsp chopped fresh dill, and salt and pepper to taste. Toss into the salad with 1 tbsp drained capers. Serve cool, garnished with sprigs of fresh dill.

● For a spicy barley salad, add a pinch of saffron strands when cooking the pearl barley and use 1 can red kidney beans, about 410 g, drained and rinsed, rather than black-eyed beans. For the dressing, whisk 1 seeded and finely chopped fresh red chilli and 2 tbsp extra virgin olive oil with the vinegar and garlic, and add chopped fresh coriander and parsley instead of the mint and chervil.

Chickpea and pitta salad

This is based on *fattoush*, the popular salad enjoyed in the Lebanon and Syria, and it makes a satisfying main dish. It's important to grill the pitta bread until it is really crisp and golden or it will quickly become soggy when mixed with the other ingredients. The dressing adds the distinctive flavours of olives, anchovy and garlic.

Serves 4

4 sesame pitta breads

2 cans chickpeas, about 410 g each, rinsed
    and drained

½ cucumber, diced

4 large beefsteak tomatoes, about 900 g
    (2 lb) in total, chopped

6 spring onions, chopped

55 g (2 oz) stoned black olives, preferably
    Kalamata olives

sprigs of fresh mint to garnish

Tapenade dressing

2 tbsp extra virgin olive oil

1 tbsp balsamic vinegar

2 tsp tapenade

1 tbsp chopped fresh mint

pepper

Preparation and cooking time: 20 minutes

Each serving provides

kcal 454, protein 18 g, fat 12 g (of which
saturated fat 2 g), carbohydrate 72 g (of
which sugars 11 g), fibre 10 g

✓✓✓	C, E
✓✓	A, B$_1$, niacin, copper, iron, potassium, zinc
✓	B$_6$, folate, calcium

1 Preheat the grill to high. Split the pitta breads in half by carefully cutting them open with a sharp knife. Toast under the grill until golden brown and crisp, turning once, then leave to cool. Tear into bite-sized pieces.

2 Put the chickpeas, cucumber, tomatoes, spring onions and olives in a serving bowl. For the dressing, whisk together the olive oil, vinegar, tapenade, mint and pepper to taste. Drizzle over the vegetables and toss together.

3 Just before serving, add the pieces of pitta bread and mix well. Serve garnished with sprigs of fresh mint.

Some more ideas

● If you cannot find sesame pitta bread you can use plain white or wholemeal pitta breads.

● Instead of adding pieces of toasted pitta bread, try polenta croutons. Bring 750 ml (1¼ pints) vegetable stock to the boil and add 170 g (6 oz) instant polenta in a steady stream, stirring. Cook for 4–5 minutes, or according to packet instructions, until the mixture is thick and pulling away from the sides of the pan. Stir in 15 g (½ oz) freshly grated Parmesan cheese, 3 tbsp chopped fresh coriander, and salt and pepper to taste. Quickly spread the polenta in a greased 18 x 28 cm (7 x 11 in) shallow tin and leave to cool for about 30 minutes or until set. Then turn out and cut into 1 cm (½ in) cubes.

Spread out the polenta croutons on a sheet of foil on the rack of the grill pan and toast under a preheated moderate grill for 5–8 minutes, turning them several times. Add two-thirds of the polenta croutons to the salad and toss well. Scatter over the remaining croutons and serve.

● Make a chickpea and aubergine salad, which is delicious either with the pitta breads or the polenta croutons. Cut a 340 g (12 oz) aubergine into 1 cm (½ in) cubes and gently fry in 2 tbsp extra virgin olive oil for 5 minutes. Stir in 1 tsp cumin seeds and continue cooking until the aubergine is lightly browned and tender. Tip into a bowl and mix with 2 cans chickpeas, about 410 g each, drained and rinsed, 1 thinly sliced red onion, 170 g (6 oz) baby spinach leaves and 1 seeded and thinly sliced yellow pepper. For the dressing, whisk together 1 tbsp extra virgin olive oil, 2 tsp lemon juice, 2 tbsp chopped fresh coriander and pepper to taste.

Plus points

● Although olives have a relatively high fat content, it is mainly unsaturated fat, which is considered to be the healthiest kind of fat to include in the diet.

● Both the white bulb and the green leaves of spring onions can be eaten. Using the green leaves increases the amount of beta-carotene that is consumed.

Puy lentils with redcurrants

Puy lentils have a delicate taste and texture and hold their shape during cooking, which makes them particularly good in salads. A combination of sweet peaches and sharp redcurrants complements them beautifully in this light, summery dish. Serve as an accompaniment to grilled fish or chicken.

Serves 4

200 g (7 oz) Puy lentils

strip of orange or lemon zest

1 bay leaf

1 tbsp raspberry vinegar

150 g (5½ oz) redcurrants

1 tsp clear honey

1 tbsp sunflower oil

2 tsp hazelnut oil

3 firm, ripe peaches, halved, stoned and thickly sliced

200 g (7 oz) mixed salad leaves such as rocket, batavia or baby spinach

salt and pepper

Preparation and cooking time: 25–30 minutes

1 Put the lentils in a saucepan, add the strip of orange or lemon zest and the bay leaf, and cover with plenty of cold water. Bring to the boil, then reduce the heat and simmer gently for 15–20 minutes or until just tender but still firm to the bite. Drain thoroughly and discard the citrus zest and bay leaf. Put the lentils in a large bowl.

2 Combine the raspberry vinegar, redcurrants and honey in a small saucepan and add 3 tbsp water. Bring to the boil and bubble for a few seconds, then remove from the heat. Lift out the redcurrants with a draining spoon and add to the lentils.

3 Whisk the sunflower and hazelnut oils into the redcurrant juices in the pan, and season with salt and pepper to taste. Drizzle this dressing over the lentils and redcurrants.

4 Add the peaches to the bowl and toss together very gently, taking care not to break up the redcurrants and peaches too much.

5 Arrange the salad leaves around the edge of a serving dish. Spoon the fruit and lentil salad into the middle and serve at room temperature.

Some more ideas

● Use other soft fruit such as blueberries instead of the redcurrants, and nectarines instead of peaches.

● For a garlicky green lentil salad, put 200 g (7 oz) green lentils in a saucepan, cover with plenty of cold water and bring to the boil. Simmer for 20–30 minutes or until tender. Drain well and tip into a bowl. Add 1 seeded and diced orange pepper, 1 chopped courgette, 4 chopped tomatoes and 2 sliced celery sticks. For the dressing, whisk 2 crushed garlic cloves with 1 tsp sun-dried tomato paste, 2 tbsp extra virgin olive oil, 2 tsp sherry vinegar and seasoning. Toss the dressing with the lentils and vegetables, and serve at room temperature.

Plus points

● Like other pulses, lentils provide fibre. They are also a good source of vitamins B_1 and niacin, both essential for helping the release of energy from food.

● Although mainly used in preserves and puddings and as a garnish, redcurrants can make a delightful addition to a savoury dish. They are a useful source of vitamin C, although nowhere near as rich in this vitamin as blackcurrants – weight for weight, they contain only a fifth of the amount present in blackcurrants.

Each serving provides

Ⓥ

kcal 252, protein 15 g, fat 7 g (of which saturated fat 1 g), carbohydrate 35 g (of which sugars 11 g), fibre 8 g

✓✓✓	A, C, copper, selenium
✓✓	folate, iron, potassium, zinc
✓	B_1, B_2, B_6, E, niacin, calcium

for maximum vitality

Oriental sprouted salad

The Chinese-style dressing for this vibrant side salad, with zesty tones of ginger and coriander, complements the fresh flavours of sprouted beans and seeds, apple and vegetables. It's easy to sprout beans and seeds at home in jars – just soak overnight, then rinse daily until the sprouts appear (see page 23 for full instructions).

Serves 4

1 carrot

1 celery stick

1 Cox's apple

100 g (3½ oz) mung bean sprouts

50 g (1¾ oz) sprouted sunflower seeds

45 g (1½ oz) sprouted alfalfa seeds

Oriental dressing

1 tbsp lime juice

1 tbsp finely chopped fresh coriander

2 tbsp sunflower oil

½ tsp toasted sesame oil

½ tsp light soy sauce

1 tsp grated fresh root ginger

salt and pepper

Preparation time: 10 minutes

1 Cut the carrot into 4 cm (1½ in) lengths. Slice thinly lengthways, then cut into very fine matchsticks. Cut the celery into matchsticks the same size as the carrot. Core the apple and cut into 8 wedges, then thinly slice the wedges crossways to make fan-shaped pieces.

2 Combine the carrot, celery, apple, mung bean sprouts and sprouted seeds in a mixing bowl.

3 To make the dressing, whisk together all the ingredients, seasoning with salt and pepper to taste. Pour the dressing over the salad, toss well to coat evenly and serve.

Some more ideas

• If you don't have time to sprout your own beans and seeds, you can use sprouts bought from supermarkets and healthfood shops. Look for bags of mixtures such as sprouted aduki beans, lentils and chickpeas.

• For a more substantial salad, to serve as a light main dish, replace the mung bean sprouts with sprouted green or brown lentils, and stir in 100 g (3½ oz) diced tofu.

• Make a sprouted salad with broccoli and orange. Blanch 100 g (3½ oz) thinly sliced broccoli florets in boiling water for 2 minutes, then drain and refresh in cold water. Peel and segment 1 large orange, and cut the segments in half. Put the broccoli and orange segments in a bowl with 150 g (5½ oz) sprouted chickpeas and 50 g (1¾ oz) sprouted wholewheat grains. For the dressing, whisk together 1½ tbsp orange juice, 2 tbsp sunflower oil, 1 tbsp snipped fresh chives, ½ tsp wholegrain mustard and seasoning to taste.

Plus points

• It is important for vegetarians and vegans to include as wide a mix of pulses, seeds and nuts as possible in their diet to make sure it contains a nutritious balance of proteins.

• Sprouted beans and seeds are a good source of vitamin C and folate, as well as several phytochemicals including lutein, coumarins and xanthophylls.

• Carrots are one of the richest sources of beta-carotene, which is essential for good night vision. The amount of beta-carotene in carrots depends on their variety and age. Older and darker orange carrots contain more than young, pale orange ones.

Each serving provides

kcal 156, **protein** 4 g, **fat** 12 g (of which saturated fat 1 g), **carbohydrate** 8 g (of which sugars 5 g), **fibre** 2 g

✓✓　A, copper

✓　B$_1$, E, iron, selenium, zinc

for maximum vitality

Carrot and radish rice salad with tofu dressing

Brown rice tossed with crisp vegetables and fresh and dried fruit makes this unusual side salad. The almost fat-free dressing is based on tofu, a curd made from soya beans, which gives it a grainy texture similar to the delicious Greek dip, hummus. For a smoother mayonnaise-like texture, use silken tofu.

Serves 4

200 g (7 oz) long-grain brown rice

125 g (4½ oz) radishes, sliced

1 large carrot, cut into matchsticks

2 spring onions, chopped

1 Asian pear, peeled, cored and diced

55 g (2 oz) raisins

4 tbsp coarsely chopped fresh coriander

Tofu dressing

125 g (4½ oz) tofu, diced

2 tsp Dijon mustard

1 tbsp white wine vinegar

1 garlic clove, crushed

3 tbsp orange juice

salt and pepper

Preparation and cooking time: 50 minutes, plus cooling

Each serving provides Ⓥ

kcal 277, **protein** 7 g, **fat** 3 g (of which saturated fat 0.5 g), **carbohydrate** 58 g (of which sugars 17 g), **fibre** 3 g

✓✓✓	A, copper
✓✓	calcium
✓	B₁, C, E, folate, niacin, iron, potassium, zinc

1 Put the rice in a saucepan, add 600 ml (1 pint) water and bring to the boil. Cover and simmer very gently for 30–40 minutes or until the rice is tender and has absorbed all the water. Remove from the heat and leave to cool.

2 While the rice is cooling, make the dressing. Put the tofu into a blender or food processor, add the mustard, vinegar, garlic and orange juice, and blend until smooth. Season with salt and pepper to taste.

3 Pour the tofu dressing into a large bowl. Add the radishes, carrot, spring onions, Asian pear, raisins and chopped coriander, and stir until well combined, then stir in the rice. Serve at room temperature or lightly chilled.

Some more ideas

● Use a ripe but firm dessert pear instead of an Asian pear. There is no need to peel it.

● To make a courgette and orange rice salad, use long-grain white rice instead of brown; this will need only 500 ml (17 fl oz) water and 10–15 minutes cooking. Make the tofu dressing as in the main recipe, adding ½ tsp grated orange zest. Stir in 1 large orange, peeled and segmented, 2 sliced celery sticks, 1 diced red pepper, 3 sliced baby courgettes and 2 tbsp snipped fresh chives, then stir in the rice.

Plus points

● Tofu is high in protein, but low in fat. It is also rich in iron and B vitamins and is a useful source of calcium.

● Like many other salad ingredients, radishes are a useful source of vitamin C, and low in calories. A mustard-type oil present in radishes gives them their hot flavour.

● Asian pears, or nashi, are large yellow-skinned fruits with crisp, scented flesh that tastes more like an apple than a pear. They are a useful source of vitamin C.

Rice and Bean Feasts

Hearty main dishes for all occasions

Take advantage of the wide variety of cereal grains and pulses to make exciting and wholesome meals for family and friends. Wrap a creamy bean mixture in flour tortillas with cheese and shredded lettuce and serve with a fresh salsa. Simmer beef with pot barley and red wine until meltingly tender, or make a classic French cassoulet with white beans, lean pork and garlicky sausage. Top borlotti beans in a wild mushroom sauce with heavenly Parmesan polenta, or use polenta to make an unusual pizza base. Try a turkey biryani or a duck risotto. Or what about crisp filo parcels filled with spicy chickpeas and feta?

Slow-braised beef and barley

Juniper berries give this dish a distinctive flavour. The beef is slowly simmered until meltingly tender, while nourishing pot barley soaks up some of the juices and thickens the rich gravy to make a hearty casserole. Serve with mashed potatoes and a green vegetable such as French beans or spring greens.

Serves 4

500 g (1 lb 2 oz) beef chuck or lean braising steak, trimmed and cut into 5 cm (2 in) cubes

2 garlic cloves, halved

3 bay leaves

6 juniper berries, lightly crushed

1 sprig of fresh thyme

250 ml (8½ fl oz) full-bodied red wine

12 button onions, about 400 g (14 oz) in total

1 tbsp extra virgin olive oil

55 g (2 oz) pot barley

400 ml (14 fl oz) beef stock

3 large carrots, cut into large chunks, about 425 g (15 oz) in total

2 celery sticks, sliced

300 g (10½ oz) swede, cut into 4 cm (1½ in) chunks

salt and pepper

Preparation time: 20 minutes, plus 8 hours marinating

Cooking time: 2–2¼ hours

Each serving provides

kcal 367, protein 31 g, fat 10 g (of which saturated fat 3 g), carbohydrate 29 g (of which sugars 18 g), fibre 8 g

✓✓✓	A
✓✓	C
✓	B₁, B₆, E, folate, niacin, calcium, copper, iron, potassium, zinc

1 Put the beef in a bowl with the garlic, bay leaves, juniper berries and thyme. Pour over the wine, then cover and leave to marinate in the fridge for 8 hours or overnight.

2 The next day, preheat the oven to 160°C (325°F, gas mark 3). Put the button onions in a bowl and pour over enough boiling water to cover. Leave for 2 minutes, then drain. When cool enough to handle, peel off the skins. Set the onions aside.

3 Remove the beef from the marinade and pat dry on kitchen paper. Heat the oil in a large flameproof casserole over a moderately high heat. Add the beef and brown on all sides. Do this in batches, if necessary, so the pan is not overcrowded. Remove the beef from the casserole and set aside on a plate.

4 Add the onions to the casserole and cook gently for 3–4 minutes or until lightly coloured all over. Add the barley and cook for 1 minute, stirring, then return the beef and any beefy juices to the casserole. Pour in the stock and bring to a simmer.

5 Strain the marinade into the casserole, and add the bay leaves and sprig of thyme. Season with salt and pepper to taste. Cover with a tight-fitting lid, transfer to the oven and braise for 45 minutes.

6 Add the carrots, celery and swede, and stir to mix. Cover again and braise for a further 1–1¼ hours or until the beef, barley and vegetables are tender. Remove the bay leaves and thyme stalk before serving.

Plus points

- Pot barley retains the outer layers of the grain (these are removed in the milling of pearl barley), and it therefore contains all the nutrients of the whole grain.
- The barley grain contains gummy fibres called beta-glucans, which appear to have significant cholesterol-lowering properties.
- Beef is an excellent source of iron, both in terms of the quantity that is present and the efficient way it is absorbed by the body.

Some more ideas

• The gravy will be quite thick. If you prefer it slightly thinner, stir in an extra 120 ml (4 fl oz) beef stock 20 minutes before the end of the cooking time.

• For slow-braised lamb and barley, use lean boneless stewing lamb instead of beef, and marinate overnight in 250 ml (8½ fl oz) dry cider mixed with 2 tsp Dijon mustard, 1 tsp molasses and 1 tsp Demerara sugar. Dry and fry the lamb as for the beef in the main recipe. Add 1 sliced onion to the casserole and cook for 4–5 minutes or until beginning to colour, then add the barley and stir for 1 minute. Pour in 250 ml (8½ fl oz) lamb or vegetable stock, 150 ml (5 fl oz) tomato juice and the marinade, and add a sprig of fresh rosemary. Cover and braise for 45 minutes. Stir in 250 g (8½ oz) baby carrots and 250 g (8½ oz) halved or quartered small turnips. Braise for a further 1–1¼ hours or until everything is tender.

Roast vegetable and bean stew

This easy, one-pot dish of root vegetables and pinto beans makes a nourishing winter main course, and needs no accompaniments. It's particularly enjoyable with a glass of dry cider or apple juice.

Serves 4

1 acorn squash, about 600 g (1 lb 5 oz)

500 g (1 lb 2 oz) new potatoes, scrubbed and cut into 4 cm (1½ in) chunks

200 g (7 oz) carrots, cut into 4 cm (1½ in) chunks

200 g (7 oz) parsnips, cut into 4 cm (1½ in) chunks

2 large courgettes, about 400 g (14 oz) in total, cut into 4 cm (1½ in) chunks

2 tbsp extra virgin olive oil

1 garlic clove, finely chopped

4 large sprigs of fresh rosemary, plus extra sprigs to garnish

2 cans pinto beans, about 410 g each, drained and rinsed

240 ml (8 fl oz) dry cider

240 ml (8 fl oz) hot vegetable stock

salt and pepper

Preparation time: 20 minutes
Cooking time: 50–55 minutes

1 Preheat the oven to 200°C (400°C, gas mark 6). Halve the squash and remove the seeds and fibres, then cut off the hard skin and cut the flesh into 4 cm (1½ in) chunks.

2 Put the squash in a bowl and add the potatoes, carrots, parsnips and courgettes. Drizzle over the olive oil and toss to coat the vegetables evenly. Stir in the garlic and season with salt and pepper to taste.

3 Lay the rosemary sprigs on the bottom of a large roasting tin and spread the vegetables on top in a single layer. Roast for about 30 minutes, turning once, until lightly browned.

4 Remove from the oven and stir in the pinto beans, cider and stock. Cover the tin tightly with foil, then return to the oven and cook for a further 20–25 minutes or until the vegetables are tender. Before serving, remove the rosemary stalks and garnish with fresh rosemary sprigs.

Some more ideas

● You can also cook the stew on top of the stove. Heat the oil in a large saucepan, add the vegetables and fry for 4–5 minutes, stirring, then add the garlic, rosemary and seasoning. Stir in the beans, cider and stock, and bring to the boil. Cover and simmer for 30–35 minutes or until tender.

● Replace the acorn squash with butternut squash and use canned ful medames beans instead of the pinto beans. Omit the potatoes from the stew and reduce the stock to 150 ml (5 fl oz). Bake 4 medium-sized potatoes in their jackets alongside the stew for 40–50 minutes or until tender. Serve the stew spooned into the split jacket potatoes.

Plus points

● Parsnips are a very nutritious starchy vegetable, providing useful amounts of potassium, the B vitamins B_1 and folate, and vitamin C.

● Use freshly dug potatoes whenever possible, as they can contain as much as 10 times more vitamin C than potatoes that have been stored.

Each serving provides

Ⓥ

kcal 452, **protein** 17 g, **fat** 8 g (of which saturated fat 1 g), **carbohydrate** 76 g (of which sugars 13 g), **fibre** 9 g

✓✓✓	A, B_1, B_6, C, folate, copper, potassium
✓✓	calcium, iron, zinc
✓	E, niacin, selenium

rice and bean feasts

Flageolet bean and lentil lasagne

This colourful main dish is built up with layers of red pepper, lentil and bean sauce, sheets of lasagne and sliced artichoke hearts. The creamy, richly flavoured topping is a combination of ricotta and Parmesan cheeses.

Serves 6

200 g (7 oz) no-precook lasagne sheets, about 12

1 can artichoke hearts in water, about 400 g, drained, rinsed and sliced

150 g (5½ oz) ricotta cheese

100 ml (3½ fl oz) semi-skimmed milk

3 tbsp freshly grated Parmesan cheese

Lentil and bean sauce

1 tbsp sunflower oil

1 large red onion, thinly sliced

100 g (3½ oz) split red lentils

2 large red peppers, seeded and diced

1 large carrot, thinly sliced

2 celery sticks, thinly sliced

550 ml (18 fl oz) vegetable stock

1 bay leaf

2 cans flageolet beans, about 410 g each, drained and rinsed

salt and pepper

Preparation time: 45 minutes, plus 5 minutes standing

Cooking time: 40 minutes

Each serving provides Ⓥ

kcal 400, **protein** 21 g, **fat** 8 g (of which saturated fat 3 g), **carbohydrate** 65 g (of which sugars 15 g), **fibre** 11 g

✓✓✓	A, C
✓✓	B₁, niacin, calcium, copper, iron, potassium, zinc
✓	B₂, B₆, E, folate, selenium

1 To make the sauce, heat the oil in a saucepan, add the onion and cook gently for 10 minutes or until softened. Add the lentils, red peppers, carrot, celery, stock and bay leaf. Bring to the boil, then reduce the heat and simmer for about 25 minutes or until the lentils and vegetables are very tender.

2 Remove the bay leaf, then purée in a blender or food processor, or using a hand-held blender directly in the pan, until smooth. Season with salt and pepper to taste, and stir in the flageolet beans.

3 Preheat the oven to 190°C (375°F, gas mark 5). Spoon about one-quarter of the sauce over the bottom of a greased large ovenproof dish. Cover with one-third of the lasagne sheets, then top with half of the remaining sauce. Arrange half the sliced artichoke hearts over the sauce. Repeat with another layer of pasta, then the rest of the sauce and the rest of the artichokes. Finish with the last of the pasta sheets.

4 Put the ricotta cheese into a bowl and stir in the milk until smooth. Season with pepper to taste. Spoon the ricotta sauce over the lasagne, then scatter the grated Parmesan on top.

5 Bake for 40 minutes or until bubbling and the top is golden. Remove from the oven and leave to stand for 5 minutes before serving.

Some more ideas

● Replace the artichoke hearts with 400 g (14 oz) baby spinach leaves, steamed for about 1 minute or until wilted.

● For a mixed bean and lentil lasagne, replace the flageolet beans with 2 cans mixed beans (usually haricot, pinto, kidney, chickpea, flageolet and soya), about 410 g each, drained and rinsed. Use either artichoke hearts or steamed spinach.

Plus points

● Red lentils cook quickly to a purée and so are particularly good in soups and sauces such as this one. Although split lentils are less nutritious than whole lentils, they still provide B vitamins and iron.

● Pasta is an excellent source of low-fat starchy carbohydrate and contains valuable vitamins, particularly the B vitamins, which help in the release of energy from food.

● Peppers contain the antioxidant beta-carotene, but the amount depends very much on the colour of the pepper. Green peppers supply 265 mcg beta-carotene per 100 g (3½ oz), while red peppers offer a whopping 3840 mcg for the same weight.

Refried bean burritos

Pinto beans often feature in Mexican cooking, as their creamy texture makes them the perfect partner for strong flavours and spices. The beans aren't actually fried twice here, but are simmered first, then cooked gently in a little oil. Burritos make a hearty meal, needing no accompaniment and perhaps just some fruit to follow.

Serves 6

250 g (8½ oz) dried pinto beans, soaked for at least 8 hours

2 onions (1 quartered and 1 finely chopped)

3 garlic cloves (2 whole and 1 finely chopped)

2 bay leaves

1½ tbsp sunflower oil

salt and pepper

Tomato and chilli salsa

450 g (1 lb) firm, ripe tomatoes, diced

1 fresh green chilli, seeded and finely chopped

finely grated zest and juice of 1 lime

pinch of caster sugar

3 tbsp chopped fresh coriander

To serve

8 large flour tortillas

115 g (4 oz) Wensleydale cheese, grated

1 cos lettuce, shredded

125 g (4½ oz) Greek-style yogurt

Preparation and cooking time: 1¾ hours, plus 8 hours soaking

Each serving provides Ⓥ

kcal 519, **protein** 22 g, **fat** 12 g (of which saturated fat 5 g), **carbohydrate** 83 g (of which sugars 8 g), **fibre** 4 g

✓✓✓	folate, copper
✓✓	A, B$_1$, E, niacin, calcium, iron, potassium, zinc
✓	B$_2$, B$_6$, C, selenium

1 Drain the soaked beans and rinse under cold running water. Put them in a large pan, cover with plenty of fresh water and add the quartered onion, 2 peeled garlic cloves and the bay leaves. Bring to the boil and boil rapidly for 10 minutes, then reduce the heat, partly cover and simmer gently for 45–60 minutes or until tender.

2 Meanwhile, make the salsa by mixing together the tomatoes, chilli, lime zest and juice, sugar and coriander in a bowl. Cover and leave at room temperature until ready to serve.

3 When the beans have finished cooking, spoon out 150 ml (5 fl oz) of the cooking liquid and reserve. Drain the beans, discarding the onion and bay leaves but reserving the garlic.

4 Heat the oil in a large frying pan, add the finely chopped onion and garlic, and cook gently for 10 minutes or until soft. Add the reserved whole garlic cloves, a ladleful of the beans and a few spoonfuls of the reserved cooking liquid. Mash with a fork to break up the beans and garlic cloves.

5 Continue adding the beans a ladleful at a time with a little of the liquid, cooking over a low heat and mashing, to make a dryish, slightly textured purée. Season with salt and pepper to taste.

6 Meanwhile, heat the tortillas in the oven or in a microwave according to the packet instructions.

7 Spoon the refried beans into the middle of the tortillas. Sprinkle with the cheese followed by the shredded lettuce, then add the yogurt. Roll up the tortillas to enclose the filling and serve immediately, with the tomato and chilli salsa.

Plus points

- Tortillas, a part of the staple diet in Mexico and other countries in Central and South America, may be made from wheat or from masa harina, a form of maize. Both types provide starchy carbohydrate, and make a great alternative to bread.

- Vitamin C supplied by the tomatoes and lime juice in the salsa helps the absorption of the iron from the pinto beans.

Another idea

- To make refried bean quesadillas, coarsely grate 200 g (7 oz) Monterey Jack, Wensleydale or mild Cheddar cheese. Heat a large frying pan or griddle over a moderately low heat. Take one of 8 large flour tortillas, place it in the pan and spoon 2–3 tbsp of the refried beans in the middle. Sprinkle one-eighth of the cheese over the bean purée and around the edge of the tortilla. Fold the tortilla over the filling to make a half-moon shape and press the edges together gently, so that the melting cheese seals them. Cook for 1 minute, then turn over and cook the other side for 1 minute. Remove from the pan and serve immediately or the cheese will become chewy. Alternatively, you can fill and fold the tortillas ahead of time, then cook them to order. Serve with a mango salsa made by mixing 1 finely chopped ripe mango with 2 seeded and sliced fresh chillies (1 green and 1 red) and the juice of ½ lime.

Quinoa with griddled aubergines

Quinoa, a nutritious grain from South America, has a texture rather like split lentils when cooked. It makes a great alternative to rice. Here it is combined with griddled aubergines, peppers, cherry tomatoes and onions, and then baked with tangy goat's cheese on the top. Serve with a mixed leaf salad.

Serves 4

300 g (10½ oz) quinoa

3–4 sprigs of fresh thyme

1.2 litres (2 pints) vegetable stock

250 g (8½ oz) baby aubergines, cut lengthways into quarters

1 red pepper, seeded and cut into chunks

1 red onion, cut into chunks

2 tbsp extra virgin olive oil

200 g (7 oz) cherry tomatoes

2 garlic cloves, crushed

300 ml (10 fl oz) tomato juice

200 g (7 oz) goat's cheese log with herbs, cut into 8 slices

salt and pepper

Preparation time: 35 minutes

Cooking time: 35 minutes

Each serving provides (V)

kcal 438, protein 20 g, fat 18 g (of which saturated fat 6.5 g), carbohydrate 53 g (of which sugars 14 g), fibre 3 g

✓✓✓ A, C, copper

✓✓ B₂, B₁₂, niacin, calcium, iron, potassium, zinc

✓ B₁, B₆, E, folate

1 Preheat the oven to 190°C (375°F, gas mark 5). Put the quinoa in a sieve and rinse thoroughly under cold running water. Place in a saucepan with the thyme sprigs and stock, and bring to the boil. Cover and simmer gently for 20 minutes or until all the stock has been absorbed and the quinoa is tender.

2 Meanwhile, heat a ridged cast-iron grill pan. Brush the aubergines, red pepper and onion with the olive oil, then cook them on the grill pan (in batches if necessary) for 4–5 minutes or until softened and lightly charred on both sides. Transfer to a plate.

3 Put the whole tomatoes on the grill pan and cook for about 2 minutes or until they are just beginning to burst their skins. Remove from the heat.

4 When the quinoa is cooked, tip it into an ovenproof dish. Add the griddled vegetables, garlic and tomato juice, and season with salt and pepper to taste. Fold together gently.

5 Arrange the slices of goat's cheese on top of the quinoa mixture. Cover with foil and bake for 35 minutes or until the vegetable are tender. Serve hot.

Some more ideas

• Instead of goat's cheese, use a log-shaped cow's milk soft cheese with garlic and herbs, slicing it or crumbling it coarsely.

• Try quinoa with fresh tuna. Marinate 2 fresh tuna steaks, about 300 g (10½ oz) in total, in 1 tbsp extra virgin olive oil, the grated zest of 1 lemon and ¼ tsp crushed dried chillies. Meanwhile, brush 125 g (4½ oz) asparagus tips and 2 courgettes, sliced on the diagonal, with 2 tbsp extra virgin olive oil and cook on the grill pan for about 30 seconds on each side. Griddle the cherry tomatoes as in the main recipe. Place the tuna on the grill pan and cook for 2 minutes on each side. Combine the quinoa, vegetables, garlic and tomato juice in an ovenproof dish, adding a handful of torn fresh basil leaves. Break the tuna into pieces and scatter over the top, pushing it down slightly. Cover with foil and bake for 25 minutes.

Plus points

• Quinoa is not a typical cereal – it produces large quantities of small seeds – but it is used like other grains. Low in fat and high in starchy carbohydrate, it has a higher protein content than other grains.

• Aubergines are filling and satisfying without adding many calories – just 15 kcals per 100 g (3½ oz).

• Goat's cheese, like other cheeses, is a good source of protein and calcium, but has a lower fat content than many other more traditional cheeses.

Cassoulet

A warming winter combination of haricot beans, cubes of pork and spicy garlic sausage, and lots of vegetables makes this classic country dish from south-west France a real winner. It is full of rich flavours and, in traditional fashion, is topped with a breadcrumb crust. Serve simply with a green salad to follow.

Serves 4

150 g (5½ oz) dried haricot beans, soaked for
    at least 8 hours
1 tbsp extra virgin olive oil
280 g (10 oz) pork fillet (tenderloin), cut into
    2.5 cm (1 in) dice
85 g (3 oz) coarse-cut, dry-cured garlicky
    French sausage, diced
1 onion, chopped
2 celery sticks, chopped
2 carrots, thickly sliced
1 turnip, chopped
1 can chopped tomatoes, about 400 g
150 ml (5 fl oz) dry white wine
400 ml (14 fl oz) pork or chicken stock
1 tbsp tomato purée
2 bay leaves
4 sprigs of fresh thyme
salt and pepper

Breadcrumb crust

1 tbsp extra virgin olive oil
85 g (3 oz) fresh white breadcrumbs
15 g (½ oz) parsley, chopped

Preparation time: 1½ hours, plus 8 hours
    soaking
Cooking time: 1¾ hours

1 Drain the soaked beans and rinse under cold running water. Put in a saucepan, cover with plenty of fresh water and bring to the boil. Boil rapidly for 10 minutes, then partly cover and simmer for 50–60 minutes or until tender. Drain and set aside.

2 Heat the oil in a large flameproof casserole, add the pork fillet and cook over a moderately high heat for 5–6 minutes or until browned. Remove with a draining spoon and set aside. Add the sausage to the casserole and brown lightly. Remove with a draining spoon and set aside with the pork.

3 Add the onion, celery, carrots and turnip to the casserole and cook for 5 minutes, stirring occasionally, until softened and lightly browned.

4 Return the pork and sausage to the casserole. Add the beans, tomatoes with their juice, the wine, stock, tomato purée, bay leaves and thyme. Bring to the boil, then reduce the heat, cover and simmer for 1½ hours or until the meat and vegetables are very tender.

5 Just before serving, prepare the breadcrumb crust. Heat the olive oil in a frying pan, add the breadcrumbs and parsley, and cook over a moderate heat, stirring constantly, for 3–4 minutes or until the crumbs are lightly golden and quite dry.

6 Taste the cassoulet and season with salt and pepper. Scatter the breadcrumb mixture evenly over the top and serve immediately.

Plus points

• Haricot beans provide protein in casseroles and stews such as this classic dish, which means the amount of meat used can be quite modest.

• Lean pork has a lower fat content than beef or lamb. It is a good source of zinc and it provides useful amounts of iron.

• Turnips contain the B vitamins B_6 and niacin as well as vitamin C in useful quantities.

Each serving provides

kcal 434, **protein** 31 g, **fat** 14 g (of which saturated fat 3 g), **carbohydrate** 42 g (of which sugars 12 g), **fibre** 10 g

✓✓✓	A
✓✓	C, calcium, copper, iron, potassium
✓	B_1, B_6, E, folate, niacin, selenium, zinc

Some more ideas

- For a really crisp breadcrumb crust, put the casserole under the grill to brown lightly.
- This is a great dish to make in advance for easy entertaining or family meals. Before serving, reheat thoroughly, then scatter over the herby breadcrumbs.

- Instead of pork fillet and garlicky sausage, use cubes of lean lamb fillet and 2–3 herby or spicy fresh pork or lamb sausages.
- To make a vegetarian cassoulet, omit the pork and sausage, use vegetable stock and increase the quantity of beans to 300 g (10½ oz). Use a variety of beans, such as

haricot, borlotti and flageolet. In step 4, simmer for 45 minutes, adding 250 g (8½ oz) shelled fresh broad beans for the last 10 minutes of the cooking time. For the topping, cook 55 g (2 oz) pine nuts with the breadcrumbs and parsley, then remove from the heat and stir in 30 g (1 oz) freshly grated Parmesan cheese.

Oaty red lentil gratin

Red lentils are mixed with chestnut mushrooms and celery to form the base of this hearty gratin. The Double Gloucester cheese and oat topping becomes lightly browned and crunchy during the few minutes in the oven. Serve with a tomato salad and green vegetables, such as broccoli and courgettes.

Serves 4

2 tbsp extra virgin olive oil

1 onion, chopped

2 celery sticks, chopped

200 g (7 oz) chestnut mushrooms, sliced

250 g (8½ oz) split red lentils

600 ml (1 pint) vegetable stock

100 g (3½ oz) rolled oats

100 g (3½ oz) Double Gloucester cheese, grated

pinch of cayenne pepper

salt and pepper

Preparation time: 45 minutes

Cooking time: 10 minutes

1 Heat the oil in a saucepan over a moderate heat, add the onion and celery, and cook, stirring occasionally, for 5 minutes.

2 Add the sliced mushrooms and stir well to combine. Cook for about 5 minutes longer or until softened.

3 Stir in the lentils and add 500 ml (17 fl oz) of the stock. Bring to the boil, then reduce the heat and cover. Simmer for about 20 minutes or until the lentils are tender, adding the rest of the stock if the lentils appear to be drying out.

4 Preheat the oven to 220°C (425°F, gas mark 7). Mix the oats with the grated cheese and cayenne pepper. When the lentils are cooked, season with salt and pepper to taste. Transfer them to a shallow ovenproof dish and spread out evenly.

5 Spread the oat and cheese mixture over the top. Place the dish in the oven and bake for about 10 minutes or until the topping is crisp and golden brown. Serve hot.

Some more ideas

• Cook the onion and celery with 2 finely chopped garlic cloves and 1 tbsp chopped fresh oregano.

• In step 2, add a pinch each of curry powder and ground cumin with the mushrooms.

• To make a mixed lentil gratin, cook the onion with 1 chopped garlic clove (omit the celery). Instead of mushrooms, add 1 chopped fennel bulb and 2 sliced small leeks, and cook for about 5 minutes or until softened. Add 125 g (4½ oz) split red lentils, 125 g (4½ oz) Puy lentils and the stock, and cook as in the main recipe. Transfer to a shallow ovenproof dish and top with a mixture of 100 g (3½ oz) fresh brown breadcrumbs, 50 g (1¾ oz) freshly grated Parmesan cheese and 50 g (1¾ oz) grated Cheddar cheese. Bake as in the main recipe.

Plus points

• Lentils are one of the nutritional wonders – high in protein, starchy carbohydrate and fibre, but very low in sodium and fat.

• Chestnut mushrooms are usually larger, firmer and browner than other cultivated varieties. They also have a stronger flavour. All mushrooms provide useful amounts of some of the B vitamins.

• Rolled oats are whole oat grains that have had their husks removed and then been rolled flat, so that they retain all the nutritional value of the whole grain.

Each serving provides (V)

kcal 464, **protein** 25 g, **fat** 17 g (of which saturated fat 7 g), **carbohydrate** 55 g (of which sugars 4 g), **fibre** 6 g

✓✓✓	copper
✓✓	B₁, B₆, niacin, calcium, iron, zinc
✓	A, B₂, B₁₂, E, folate, potassium, selenium

Tuscan-style baked polenta

Polenta is the much loved 'mashed potatoes' of northern Italy, a delicious comfort food to many Italians that is now enjoyed around the world. In this recipe, Parmesan-flavoured 'soft' polenta – polenta that hasn't been left to set – provides the topping for a mixture of borlotti beans and a creamy wild mushroom sauce.

Serves 4

25 g (scant 1 oz) dried porcini mushrooms
400 ml (14 fl oz) semi-skimmed milk
1½ tbsp extra virgin olive oil
15 g (½ oz) butter
2 celery sticks, thinly sliced
250 g (8½ oz) chestnut mushrooms, sliced
3 tbsp plain flour
squeeze of lemon juice
1 can borlotti beans, about 410 g, drained
    and rinsed
170 g (6 oz) instant polenta
2 eggs, lightly beaten
30 g (1 oz) Parmesan cheese, freshly grated
salt and pepper

Preparation time: 45 minutes
Cooking time: 20 minutes

Each serving provides Ⓥ
kcal 481, protein 23 g, fat 16 g (of which saturated fat 6 g), carbohydrate 64 g (of which sugars 8 g), fibre 10 g

✓✓✓	copper
✓✓	B₂, B₁₂, niacin, calcium, potassium, selenium, zinc
✓	A, B₁, B₆, folate, iron

1 Place the dried mushrooms in a small saucepan and add 250 ml (9 fl oz) of the milk. Bring just to the boil, then remove from the heat and set aside to soak.

2 Heat the oil and butter in a wide saucepan over a moderate heat. Add the celery and cook gently, stirring occasionally, for 3–4 minutes or until softened. Raise the heat, add the mushrooms and cook, stirring, for about 3 minutes or until softened.

3 Add the flour and cook, stirring, for 2 minutes. Gradually mix in the remaining 150 ml (5 fl oz) milk and cook, stirring well, until the mixture just comes to the boil and thickens.

4 Strain the milk from the porcini mushrooms and add it to the mushroom and celery sauce. Bring back to the boil, stirring. Coarsely chop the porcini and add to the pan. Simmer for 2 minutes, then add the lemon juice and season with salt and pepper to taste.

5 Pour the mushroom sauce into a shallow ovenproof dish and spread out in an even layer. Scatter the borlotti beans on top. Set aside.

6 Preheat the oven to 200°C (400°F, gas mark 6). In a heavy-based saucepan, cook the polenta in 750 ml (1¼ pints) boiling water, or according to the packet instructions, until it is thick.

Remove from the heat and briskly stir in the eggs and about half of the grated Parmesan. Season with salt and pepper to taste.

7 Pour the polenta mixture over the mushrooms and beans. Sprinkle the remaining Parmesan cheese over the top. Bake for about 20 minutes or until the filling is bubbling and the top is lightly browned. Serve hot.

Plus points
• Polenta is very versatile: it can be served 'soft' with fish, meat and vegetable dishes as an alternative to pasta or rice, or it can be left to set, then cut up and grilled or fried. It is particularly useful for those who need to follow a wheat or gluten-free diet.
• Milk is one of our most nourishing foods, being rich in calcium and protein as well as providing many B vitamins and phosphorus.
• The oil obtained from olives is high in monounsaturated fatty acids. These healthy fats are believed to help lower blood cholesterol levels.

Some more ideas

- Replace the borlotti beans with canned pinto or cannellini beans.
- Spread 500 g (1 lb 2 oz) spinach, steamed, well drained and coarsely chopped, over the mushroom sauce before adding the beans.
- To make baked polenta with tuna, soften 2 chopped celery sticks, 2 chopped carrots and 1 chopped onion in the oil and butter. Stir in the flour, then gradually stir in 250 ml (8½ fl oz) vegetable stock and 120 ml (4 fl oz) semi-skimmed milk. Bring to the boil, stirring, and simmer for about 5 minutes. Add 2 cans tuna in spring water, about 200 g each, well drained, and stir gently, just to break up the large chunks of fish. Season with salt and pepper to taste. Prepare the polenta as in the main recipe, but omit the Parmesan. Pour the fish mixture into an ovenproof dish, cover with the polenta and sprinkle with 1 tbsp freshly grated Parmesan. Bake as in the main recipe.

Chickpea and feta parcels

Crisp, golden parcels filled with chickpeas, potatoes and cheese, with a touch of warm Eastern spices, make a really tasty and satisfying main dish. Pair them with a tomato or mixed salad, and you have a complete meal. Served cold, they would also make a great addition to a packed lunch or picnic.

Serves 4 (makes 8)

200 g (7 oz) potatoes, peeled and cut into
    1 cm (½ in) dice
5 tbsp extra virgin olive oil
6 shallots, finely chopped
1½ tsp ground coriander
1½ tsp ground cumin
2 cans chickpeas, about 410 g each, drained
    and rinsed
45 g (1½ oz) feta cheese, crumbled
45 g (1½ oz) sultanas
1 small fresh red chilli, seeded and chopped
3 tbsp snipped fresh chives
16 sheets filo pastry, about 30 x 18 cm
    (12 x 7 in) each, 280 g (10 oz) in total
1 tsp sesame seeds
salt and pepper

Preparation time: 25 minutes
Cooking time: 20–25 minutes

1 Preheat the oven to 190°C (375°F, gas mark 5). Put the potatoes in a saucepan of boiling water and simmer for 5 minutes. Drain well and set aside.

2 Heat 1 tbsp of the oil in a wide pan, add the shallots and cook gently for 2–3 minutes or until softened. Stir in the ground coriander and cumin, and cook for 30 seconds.

3 Remove from the heat and add the chickpeas, potatoes, feta, sultanas, chilli and chives. Season with salt and pepper to taste. Stir well to mix.

4 Lay a sheet of filo pastry out on a work surface and brush lightly with some of the remaining oil. Top with a second sheet and brush lightly with oil. Place one-eighth of the filling at a short end, about 2.5 cm (1 in) from the edge. Fold in the sides over the filling, then fold over the nearest edge and roll up into a neat parcel. Repeat with the remaining sheets of filo and filling to make 8 parcels.

5 Place on a baking sheet, brush lightly with the last of the oil and sprinkle with the sesame seeds. Bake for 20–25 minutes or until crisp and golden brown. Serve warm or cold.

Some more ideas

• To make curried chickpea parcels, add 2 tsp mild curry paste with the spices in step 2. If you prefer a hotter filling, leave the seeds in the chilli.

• For butter bean parcels, use 2 cans butter beans, about 410 g each, drained and rinsed, and mix with the potatoes, 4 finely chopped spring onions, 45 g (1½ oz) crumbled Cheshire cheese and 4 tbsp apple chutney. Season with salt and pepper, then wrap in the filo sheets and bake as in the main recipe.

Plus points

• Filo pastry contains no fat; it's just what you add when brushing it. Using olive oil rather than melted butter minimises the amount of saturated fat.

• Like other pulses, chickpeas are an important source of protein for those following a vegetarian diet. Combining chickpeas with dairy foods such as cheese makes a nutritionally well-balanced dish.

• Feta cheese, traditionally made from sheep's milk, is moist and crumbly. It is high in saturated fat and salt, but has such a good piquant flavour that a little can go a long way in a recipe.

Each serving provides

kcal 571, **protein** 19 g, **fat** 22 g (of which saturated fat 4 g), **carbohydrate** 79 g (of which sugars 9 g), **fibre** 6 g

✓✓   E

✓   B₁, B₆, C, folate, niacin, calcium, copper, iron, potassium, zinc

Grilled polenta and tuna pizza

Polenta is a wonderfully versatile ingredient, as is shown by this quick and simple base for pizza. On its own, polenta can be quite bland, but it is an excellent foil for other flavours such as the tuna, olives, herbs and rich tomato sauce that make up the pizza topping. Serve the pizza with a green salad.

Serves 4

340 g (12 oz) instant polenta
1 tbsp chopped fresh thyme
3 tbsp chopped parsley
1 tbsp extra virgin olive oil
1 can chopped tomatoes, about 400 g
1 yellow pepper, halved and seeded
1 can tuna in spring water, about 200 g, drained and flaked
250 g (8½ oz) ricotta cheese
12 black olives, stoned and halved
salt and pepper
1–2 tsp fresh thyme leaves to garnish

Preparation time: 30 minutes
Cooking time: 10–12 minutes

Each serving provides
kcal 504, protein 26.5 g, fat 11 g (of which saturated fat 5 g), carbohydrate 75 g (of which sugars 6 g), fibre 9 g

✓✓✓	B₁₂, C, selenium
✓✓	A, niacin, calcium
✓	B₆, E, copper, iron, potassium, zinc

1 Cook the polenta in 1.3 litres (2¼ pints) boiling water for about 5 minutes, or according to the packet instructions, until thick.

2 Remove from the heat and stir in the chopped thyme, parsley, and salt and pepper to taste. Spoon the polenta onto a greased baking sheet or pizza tin and spread out to make a smooth 30 cm (12 in) round with slightly raised edges. Brush the edges with the olive oil. Set aside.

3 Preheat the grill to high. Put the tomatoes in a saucepan with their juice and bring to the boil. Simmer over a moderate heat for 6–8 minutes, stirring occasionally, until most of the liquid has evaporated, leaving a fairly thick sauce. Season to taste.

4 Meanwhile, grill the yellow pepper, skin side up, until blistered and blackened all over. Put the pepper in a polythene bag and leave until it is cool enough to handle, then peel off the skin. Slice the pepper.

5 Spread the tomato sauce over the polenta base and top with the pepper strips, tuna, crumbled ricotta and olive halves. Turn the grill down to moderately hot and grill the pizza for 10–12 minutes or until bubbling and golden brown. Sprinkle with the thyme leaves and serve.

Some more ideas

• For a spicy ham and mushroom pizza, add ¼ tsp crushed dried chillies to the tomato sauce. Instead of the yellow pepper, sauté 150 g (5½ oz) sliced chestnut mushrooms in 2 tsp extra virgin olive oil, and replace the tuna with 100 g (3½ oz) thinly sliced cooked ham.

• To make an aubergine and onion pizza, gently fry 500 g (1 lb 2 oz) thinly sliced onions with 1 crushed garlic clove in 2 tbsp extra virgin olive oil for about 20 minutes or until very soft and lightly coloured. Spread the onions over the polenta base. Thinly slice a 250 g (8½ oz) aubergine, brush lightly with extra virgin olive oil and grill until golden on both sides. Arrange the aubergine over the onions, and sprinkle with 30 g (1 oz) chopped walnuts, 8 chopped anchovy fillets and 150 g (5½ oz) diced mozzarella. Grill as in the main recipe.

Plus points

• When tuna is canned, it retains vitamins and minerals, and some omega-3 fatty acids. Tuna canned in spring water or brine contains half the calories of tuna in oil.

• The naturally waxy skin of peppers helps to prevent the loss of vitamin C during storage. As a result, their vitamin C content remains high even several weeks after harvesting.

Steamed sea bass with black beans

In this fragrant, fresh-tasting dish, sea bass fillets are sprinkled with rice wine and steamed, then served with a Chinese-style black bean sauce flavoured with ginger, garlic and soy. Serve it with herbed brown rice.

Serves 4

115 g (4 oz) dried black beans, soaked for at least 8 hours

4 sea bass fillets, about 550 g (1¼ lb) in total, skin on

1 tbsp rice wine

1 tbsp sunflower oil

1 garlic clove, crushed

2 shallots, finely chopped

2.5 cm (1 in) piece of fresh root ginger, finely chopped

4 tbsp vegetable stock

2 tbsp light soy sauce

2 tbsp dry sherry

2 tsp soft light brown sugar

1 tsp cornflour

salt and pepper

chopped fresh coriander or flat-leaf parsley, plus sprigs, to garnish

Preparation and cooking time: 1¼ hours, plus 8 hours soaking

Each serving provides

kcal 287, **protein** 34 g, **fat** 7 g (of which saturated fat 1 g), **carbohydrate** 22 g (of which sugars 4 g), **fibre** 2.5 g

✓✓✓ B$_{12}$

✓✓ folate, calcium, iron

✓ B$_1$, E, copper, potassium, zinc

1 Drain the soaked beans and rinse under cold running water. Put them in a saucepan, cover with plenty of fresh cold water and bring to the boil. Boil rapidly for 10 minutes, then reduce the heat and simmer for 45–60 minutes or until tender. Drain well and set aside.

2 Arrange the sea bass fillets, in one layer, in a steamer. Sprinkle with the rice wine and season with salt and pepper to taste. Cover and steam for about 10 minutes, depending on the thickness of the fillets; they should be firm, opaque and just able to be flaked with the tip of a knife.

3 Meanwhile, heat the oil in a frying pan or wok, add the garlic, shallots and ginger, and stir-fry for 3–4 minutes or until softened. Add the black beans, stock, soy sauce, sherry and sugar, and stir-fry until hot and bubbling.

4 Mix the cornflour to a smooth paste with 2 tbsp water and add to the pan or wok. Bring to the boil, stirring until the sauce thickens, then simmer for 1–2 minutes, stirring frequently.

5 Put the steamed sea bass fillets on 4 serving plates. Spoon over the black bean sauce, garnish with fresh herbs and serve.

Some more ideas

● Sprinkle the fish with dry sherry, or lemon or lime juice, instead of rice wine.

● For butterflied prawns with black beans, use 340 g (12 oz) peeled raw king or tiger prawns (if you like, leave the last section of the tail shell on). To butterfly them, simply cut a deep slit along the back of each prawn without cutting all the way through, then open the prawn out flat, like a book. Lightly brush the prawns all over with 2 tsp sunflower oil and cook under a preheated hot grill for 3–4 minutes or until pink. Alternatively, stir-fry the butterflied prawns in 1 tbsp sunflower oil for 2–3 minutes. Add the hot black bean sauce to the prawns and toss briefly to mix, then serve with rice noodles.

Plus points

● Traditional versions of this Chinese-style dish are high in sodium because they use black beans that have been fermented and salted. Here, dried black beans are used instead.

● White fish like sea bass are a rich source of protein with very little fat. They are also a good source of vitamin B$_{12}$, essential for the formation of red blood cells.

● Ginger has been recognised for centuries for its medicinal properties, particularly in helping digestion and preventing nausea.

Duck and wild mushroom risotto

Risotto rice absorbs delectable flavours from dried porcini mushrooms, herbs, garlic and vegetable stock, before being tossed with sautéed fresh mushrooms and slices of tender duck to make a spectacular supper dish.

Serves 4

10 g (scant ½ oz) dried porcini mushrooms

300 ml (10 fl oz) boiling water

750 ml (1¼ pints) hot vegetable stock

2 tbsp sunflower oil

2 duck breasts, about 340 g (12 oz) in total, skinned

1 red onion, finely chopped

1 garlic clove, crushed

340 g (12 oz) risotto rice

150 ml (5 fl oz) dry white wine

1 tsp finely grated lemon zest

2 tsp chopped fresh thyme

15 g (½ oz) butter

450 g (1 lb) mixed fresh mushrooms, such as oyster mushrooms, ceps and shiitake, sliced if large

3 tbsp chopped parsley

salt and pepper

Preparation and cooking time: 1 hour, plus 20 minutes soaking and 5 minutes standing

Each serving provides

kcal 558, **protein** 27 g, **fat** 16 g (of which saturated fat 5 g), **carbohydrate** 68 g (of which sugars 3 g), **fibre** 2 g

✓✓✓	B₁₂, niacin, copper, zinc
✓✓	B₁, B₂, E, iron, potassium
✓	B₆, folate, selenium

1 Put the porcini mushrooms in a bowl and pour over the boiling water. Leave to soak for 20 minutes, then drain, reserving the soaking liquid. Finely chop the mushrooms and set aside. Strain the liquid into a saucepan. Add the stock and keep hot over a very low heat.

2 Brush 1 tsp of the oil over a ridged cast-iron grill pan and heat it. Add the duck breasts, reduce the heat to moderate and cook for 8–12 minutes, turning once, until done to your taste. Remove from the pan and leave to rest in a warm place for 10 minutes, then cut into thin slices. Keep warm.

3 Meanwhile, heat 1 tbsp of the remaining oil in a heavy-based saucepan, add the onion and garlic, and fry gently for 4–5 minutes or until softened. Add the rice and stir for about 1 minute to coat it with the oil.

4 Add the wine and bubble until it has almost all been absorbed. Stir in the lemon zest, thyme and porcini mushrooms, then add a ladleful of the stock. Bubble, stirring frequently, until it has almost all been absorbed, then add another ladleful of stock. Continue adding the stock gradually in this way – total cooking time will be 15–20 minutes. The risotto is ready when the rice is tender but still firm and the texture is moist and creamy.

5 About 5 minutes before the end of cooking time, heat the remaining 2 tsp of oil and the butter in a large frying pan. Add the fresh mushrooms and sauté over a high heat for 4 minutes or until tender.

6 Stir the mushrooms into the risotto together with the duck and any duck juices. Add the parsley and season with salt and pepper to taste. Cover the pan and leave to stand off the heat for 5 minutes before serving.

Plus points

• Removing the skin and fat from duck breasts lowers the fat content considerably: skinless duck breast contains only a little more fat than skinless chicken breast.

• Most recipes use mushrooms in such small quantities that the nutritional contribution they make to the diet is not as great as that of flavour and texture. Here a good quantity is used, which boosts the B vitamins and minerals in the dish.

• Red onions have been shown to contain higher levels of flavonoids – compounds that can help to protect against heart disease – than white onions.

Another idea

● For a clam and crab risotto, scrub 900 g (2 lb) fresh clams under cold running water, discarding any open ones that do not close when sharply tapped. Pour 150 ml (5 fl oz) dry white wine into a large saucepan and add the clams with 2 peeled garlic cloves. Cover tightly, bring to the boil over a high heat and cook for about 5 minutes, shaking the pan frequently, until the clams have opened. Tip into a colander set over a bowl. When cool enough to handle, remove the clams from their shells, discarding any that haven't opened. Strain the liquid through a fine sieve and make up to 1 litre (1¾ pints) with vegetable stock. Keep hot over a low heat. Soften 1 chopped onion in 1 tbsp extra virgin olive oil in a large saucepan. Stir in 2 chopped celery sticks, 1 thinly sliced fennel bulb and 340 g (12 oz) risotto rice. Cook for 1 minute, then add the stock as in the main recipe, a ladleful at a time. When the risotto has finished cooking, stir in the clams, 170 g (6 oz) fresh white crab meat, 2 tbsp chopped fresh dill and seasoning to taste.

Turkey biryani with raita

A biryani consists of curried meat, poultry, fish or vegetables combined with basmati rice to make a complete meal. Here a turkey curry is layered with the rice and baked, then served with a fresh cucumber raita.

Serves 4

1 tbsp sunflower oil

1 large onion, chopped

450 g (1 lb) boneless turkey thigh meat, skinned and diced

15 g (½ oz) fresh root ginger, finely chopped

1 small fresh chilli, seeded and finely chopped

seeds from 10 cardamom pods, lightly crushed

1 tbsp ground cumin

1 tbsp ground coriander

6 cloves

1 cinnamon stick

2 bay leaves

½ tsp crushed black peppercorns

1 can chopped tomatoes, about 400 g

300 ml (10 fl oz) chicken stock, or as needed

55 g (2 oz) sultanas

225 g (8 oz) basmati rice, rinsed

½ tsp turmeric

30 g (1 oz) toasted flaked almonds

salt

Cucumber raita

100 g (3½ oz) Greek-style yogurt

100 g (3½ oz) plain low-fat yogurt

½ large cucumber, coarsely grated and squeezed dry

2 tbsp chopped fresh mint

Preparation time: 1¼ hours

Cooking time: 25 minutes

1 Heat the oil in a large frying pan, add the onion and cook gently for 5 minutes or until softened. Add the turkey and cook over a moderate heat for 5 minutes or until browned all over.

2 Stir in the ginger, chilli, cardamom, cumin, coriander, cloves, cinnamon stick, bay leaves and peppercorns. Cook for 1 minute, stirring all the time to ensure the spices do not burn.

3 Add the tomatoes with their juice, stock, sultanas and a pinch of salt. Bring to the boil, then reduce the heat, cover and cook gently for 45 minutes.

4 Meanwhile, preheat the oven to 160°C (325°F, gas mark 3). Put the rice in a saucepan, add 600 ml (1 pint) water and the turmeric, and bring to the boil. Cover and simmer very gently for about 7 minutes or until the rice is almost tender. Drain off excess water.

5 Layer the turkey curry and rice in a casserole dish. Cover and cook in the oven for 25 minutes, checking after 20 minutes and adding a little more stock if needed (there should be enough liquid for the rice to complete cooking).

6 Meanwhile, make the raita. Stir together the Greek-style and low-fat yogurts, cucumber and mint. Season with a pinch of salt.

7 When the biryani is ready, stir it well, then scatter the toasted almonds on top. Serve with the raita.

Plus points

- Turkey is a good source of many of the B vitamins, including B_1, niacin and B_{12}, and zinc. Zinc is vital for normal growth, as well as for the efficient functioning of the immune system.

- Yogurt provides calcium, protein and B vitamins. Traditional Greek-style yogurt is higher in fat than plain low-fat yogurt, but mixing the two together means you reduce the total amount of fat while retaining the creaminess that Greek-style yogurt gives.

Each serving provides

kcal 518, **protein** 34 g, **fat** 13 g (of which saturated fat 3 g), **carbohydrate** 68 g (of which sugars 21 g), **fibre** 3 g

✓✓✓	B_{12}, zinc
✓✓	B_6, E, niacin, copper, potassium, selenium
✓	A, B_1, B_2, C, folate, calcium, iron

Some more ideas

• The turkey curry can be made in advance and the dish finished later by cooking the rice and baking the two together. Or, you can cook the curry uncovered so that some of the liquid evaporates, and cook the rice completely, for 10–15 minutes. Mix them without baking.

• To make a mixed bean biryani, omit the turkey and use 1 can each of chickpeas, red kidney beans and black-eyed beans, all about 410 g, drained and rinsed. Cook the onion and spice mixture as in the main recipe, then add the tomatoes, 450 ml (15 fl oz) vegetable stock, the sultanas and mixed beans. Cook gently for

15–20 minutes. Layer in a casserole with the part-cooked rice and bake.

• For a chickpea and vegetable biryani, use 2 cans chickpeas, about 410 g each, drained and rinsed. Cook as for the mixed bean biryani, adding thickly sliced new potatoes and carrots and cauliflower florets with the chickpeas.

Prawn and red mullet paella

This classic Spanish favourite is always enthusiastically welcomed at the dinner table by seafood lovers. This version is packed with colourful red and yellow peppers, asparagus and peas, together with large, succulent tiger prawns and chunks of red mullet. Serve with a green salad for a memorable Mediterranean-style meal.

Serves 4

1 tbsp extra virgin olive oil

1 large onion, roughly chopped

large pinch of saffron strands

1 red pepper, seeded and roughly chopped

1 yellow pepper, seeded and roughly chopped

2 garlic cloves, crushed

250 g (8½ oz) long-grain brown rice

100 ml (3½ fl oz) dry white wine

360 ml (12 fl oz) hot fish stock, or as needed

3–4 sprigs of fresh rosemary

2 red mullet, about 180 g (6½ oz) each, cleaned

115 g (4 oz) asparagus tips, cut in half lengthways

115 g (4 oz) frozen peas

200 g (7 oz) cooked peeled tiger prawns

salt and pepper

lemon wedges to serve

Preparation time: 20 minutes

Cooking time: about 45 minutes

Each serving provides

kcal 432, **protein** 28 g, **fat** 7 g (of which saturated fat 1 g), **carbohydrate** 64 g (of which sugars 10 g), **fibre** 5 g

✓✓✓	B$_{12}$, C, copper, selenium
✓✓	A, B$_1$, B$_6$, folate, niacin, zinc
✓	E, calcium, iron, potassium

1 Heat the olive oil in a large, deep frying pan, add the onion and cook gently for 5 minutes or until softened. Meanwhile, soak the saffron in 2 tbsp boiling water.

2 Add the peppers and garlic to the pan and cook for 3–4 minutes. Stir in the rice, then add the wine, hot stock, saffron mixture, rosemary sprigs, and salt and pepper to taste. Bring to the boil, then cover, reduce the heat and cook for 25 minutes or until the rice is almost tender, adding more stock if it is all absorbed before the rice is ready.

3 Meanwhile, preheat the grill to moderate. Place the red mullet in a shallow flameproof dish and grill for about 6 minutes on each side. To test if the fish is cooked, insert a knife tip near the bone; the flesh should flake easily. Cut off the heads and tails, remove the bones and cut the flesh (with skin) into large, bite-sized pieces.

4 Add the asparagus tips and peas to the rice and mix in. Cook, covered, for a further 5 minutes, by which time all the stock should have been absorbed and the rice should be tender.

5 Add the prawns and red mullet to the pan and stir carefully to mix them into the rice. Cover and cook gently for 4–5 minutes to heat through, then serve with lemon wedges.

Plus points

● Red mullet has lean, firm flesh with a taste more reminiscent of shellfish than white fish. It is an excellent source of selenium, a mineral with potent antioxidant properties.

● Prawns contain useful amounts of many of the B vitamins, most notably vitamin B$_{12}$, which is essential for healthy blood and nervous system.

● Fresh peas have a short season, but frozen peas can be eaten throughout the year. They have a similar nutritional content to fresh peas as long as they are not overcooked.

rice and bean feasts

Another idea

• To make braised rice with mussels, scrub 1 kg (2¼ lb) mussels under cold running water, discarding any open ones that do not close when tapped sharply. Put them in a large pan with 90 ml (3 fl oz) white wine, 1 chopped onion, 2 chopped garlic cloves and a handful of chopped parsley stalks, then cover and cook over a high heat for 3–4 minutes, shaking the pan frequently, until the shells open. Remove most of the mussels from their shells. Strain the liquid and make up to 750 ml (1¼ pints) with fish or vegetable stock. Sauté 2 chopped leeks (white part only) and 2 crushed garlic cloves in 1 tbsp extra virgin olive oil until softened. Stir in 250 g (8½ oz) long-grain white rice, then add the stock with 2 bay leaves, 2 sprigs of fresh thyme and seasoning to taste. Bring to the boil, then reduce the heat, cover and simmer for 10–15 minutes or until the rice is just tender. Add 1 can artichoke hearts, about 400 g, drained and sliced, and 115 g (4 oz) frozen petit pois and cook, covered, for a further 5 minutes. Toss in the shelled mussels, 55 g (2 oz) chopped watercress and 3 tbsp chopped parsley, and heat through. Garnish with the mussels in their shells and lemon wedges.

Spiced lamb with wholewheat

Pre-cooked wholewheat grain has been popular in France for some time and is now fast catching on in the UK. Here it is cooked with spices, dried fruits and tender lamb cutlets to make a delicious Middle Eastern-style dish.

Serves 4

4 lamb chops, about 400 g (14 oz) in total, trimmed of all fat

1 onion, chopped

2 tsp finely chopped fresh root ginger

2 tsp cumin seeds

225 g (8 oz) pre-cooked wholewheat grains

600 ml (1 pint) chicken or vegetable stock

juice of 1 orange

1 tsp clear honey

seeds from 6 cardamom pods

1 cinnamon stick

250 g (8½ oz) ready-to-eat prunes

55 g (2 oz) ready-to-eat dried apricots, cut into slivers

2 tbsp chopped fresh mint

salt and pepper

To garnish

1 orange, segmented and segments halved

30 g (1 oz) unsalted pistachio nuts, chopped

sprigs of fresh mint

Preparation time: 15 minutes

Cooking time: 30–35 minutes

Each serving provides

kcal 540, **protein** 31 g, **fat** 13 g (of which saturated fat 1 g), **carbohydrate** 76 g (of which sugars 36 g), **fibre** 9 g

✓✓✓	copper
✓✓	B₁, C, niacin, iron, potassium
✓	B₂, B₆, calcium

1 Heat a large, deep, non-stick frying pan. Add the lamb cutlets and cook over a moderate heat for 2 minutes on each side or until nicely browned. Transfer to a plate.

2 Add the onion to the juices left in the pan (there shouldn't be any need to add any oil) and cook gently for 5 minutes or until softened. Stir in the ginger and cumin seeds, and cook gently for 1 minute.

3 Stir in the wholewheat, then add the stock, orange juice, honey, cardamom seeds and cinnamon stick. Bring to the boil. Reduce the heat, and return the lamb to the pan together with the prunes, apricots, mint, and salt and pepper to taste. Cover and simmer gently for 15–20 minutes or until the wholewheat is tender and all the liquid has been absorbed.

4 Stir in the orange segments and scatter the chopped pistachio nuts over the top. Serve garnished with sprigs of mint.

Some more ideas

• Flavoured varieties of pre-cooked wholewheat are available, for example, with sun-dried tomato. This would be delicious used here.

• For a lamb pilaf with dates, cut 225 g (8 oz) lean boneless lamb (leg, shoulder or neck fillet) into small cubes. Heat 1 tbsp sunflower oil in a large frying pan, add the lamb and brown all over. Add 1 chopped onion and 2 tsp finely chopped fresh root ginger and cook for about 5 minutes or until softened. Add 1 can chopped tomatoes, about 400 g, with the juice, 450 ml (15 fl oz) lamb or chicken stock, 1 tsp each ground cumin and ground coriander, and seasoning to taste. Bring to the boil, then cover and cook gently for 15 minutes. Stir in 225 g (8 oz) basmati rice, a further 300 ml (10 fl oz) hot stock and 225 g (8 oz) stoned whole dates. Cover and cook for 10–15 minutes or until the rice is tender. Scatter over a generous handful of chopped fresh coriander and serve.

Plus points

• Lamb tends to be a fatty meat, but changes in breeding, feeding and butchery techniques have reduced the fat content considerably. Today, lean cuts contain about one-third of the fat that was found in lamb 20 years ago.

• Prunes contain useful amounts of potassium, iron and vitamin B₆. They are also a good source of dietary fibre.

Rice-stuffed squash

Here's an attractive and fun way to serve small winter squashes – filled with a mixture of wild and white rice, chestnuts, dried cranberries and mozzarella cheese. Individual squashes such as acorn, onion or gem, or small pumpkins, are all suitable. It makes an impressive vegetarian main course for a winter dinner.

Serves 4

200 g (7 oz) mixed basmati and wild rice

4 small acorn squashes, about 750 g
   (1 lb 10 oz) each

185 g (6½ oz) cooked chestnuts (canned or
   vacuum packed), roughly chopped

75 g (2½ oz) dried cranberries

1 small red onion, finely chopped

2 tbsp chopped fresh thyme

2 tbsp chopped parsley

150 g (5½ oz) mozzarella cheese, grated

salt and pepper

Preparation time: 25 minutes

Cooking time: 45 minutes

1 Put the rice in a saucepan, add 400 ml (14 fl oz) water and bring to the boil. Cover and simmer very gently for about 20 minutes or until the rice is just tender. Drain off any excess water.

2 Meanwhile, preheat the oven to 180°C (350°F, gas mark 4). Using a large, sharp knife, slice off the top quarter (stalk end) of each squash. Set aside these little hats, then scoop out the seeds and fibres from the centre of the squashes using a small spoon. Trim the bases to make them level, if necessary. Season the cavity of each squash with salt and pepper, then place them in a large ovenproof dish or roasting tin.

3 Mix together the rice, chestnuts, cranberries, onion, thyme, parsley and mozzarella in a large bowl. Season with salt and pepper to taste.

4 Spoon the rice stuffing into the squashes, pressing it down and mounding it up neatly on top. Replace the reserved 'hats' on top. Bake for about 45 minutes or until the flesh of the squash is tender when pierced with a small, sharp knife. Serve hot.

Plus points

● Acorn squash is a winter variety of squash. Winter squashes are allowed to mature into hard, starchy vegetable fruits with very good keeping properties, while varieties such as courgettes are eaten while immature and the skins are still edible. Acorn squash is a good source of beta-carotene, which the body can convert to vitamin A.

● Unlike other nuts, chestnuts are high in starchy carbohydrate and low in fat – other nuts have up to 20 times as much fat. Chestnuts are also a good source of vitamin B_1 and potassium, and a valuable source of dietary fibre.

● Both dried and fresh cranberries are a good source of vitamin C. Cranberries also have the reputation of helping to control urinary tract infections such as cystitis.

Each serving provides Ⓥ

kcal 474, **protein** 19 g, **fat** 11 g (of which saturated fat 6 g), **carbohydrate** 79 g (of which sugars 17.5 g), **fibre** 10 g

✓✓✓ A, B_1, C, E, calcium

✓✓ B_{12}, copper, iron, potassium, zinc

✓ B_6, folate, niacin

rice and bean feasts

136

Some more ideas

• Use other winter squashes such as onion squash, gem squash or small pumpkins instead of acorn squash. The cooking time can vary from 45–60 minutes, depending on the type of squash and its size.

• Replace the mozzarella with other cheeses, such as Gruyère.

• Make feta and sultana rice-stuffed peppers. Cut 2 large red and 2 large yellow peppers in half lengthways and remove the cores and seeds. Make the rice filling as in the main recipe, but replace the cranberries with sultanas and the mozzarella cheese with grated feta cheese. Using your hands, scoop the stuffing into the pepper halves, pressing it down and mounding it up neatly on top. Arrange the pepper halves, side by side, in an ovenproof dish and drizzle over a mixture of the juice of 1 large orange, 1 tbsp extra virgin olive oil and pepper to taste. Cover the dish with greased foil and bake in a preheated 190°C (375°F, gas mark 5) oven for about 1 hour or until the peppers have softened. Serve hot.

Side Dishes

Tasty and nutritious accompaniments

Rice is a versatile ingredient for side dishes, and other cereal grains such as pearl barley and millet can be used in the same way, boosting the starchy carbohydrate in a meal. Beans, too, make great partners for all kinds of main dishes. Chillied chickpea and rice balls work well in an Indian menu; so does a colourful lentil and vegetable dal. Warmly spiced basmati rice, given extra zing with fresh pomegranate, is a good partner for grilled chicken. Or you could try vibrantly coloured green herb rice. Japanese glutinous rice, tinted rosy red with aduki beans, is an unusual and exciting dish, as is a combination of millet, dried apricots, spinach and pine nuts.

Fragrant basmati rice

Basmati cooks to perfect, separate, fluffy grains and is considered by many to be the finest rice. Here it is subtly scented and coloured with saffron, cinnamon and ginger. The sweet-sharp flavour of pomegranate adds a unique quality to this dish, and a few seeds scattered over the top just before serving make an attractive finish.

Serves 6

1 tbsp sunflower oil

55 g (2 oz) split blanched almonds, any tiny pieces discarded

250 g (8½ oz) basmati rice, rinsed

pinch of saffron strands

1 cinnamon stick

450 ml (15 fl oz) boiling vegetable stock

1 ripe pomegranate

2.5 cm (1 in) piece of fresh root ginger, grated

1 tsp clear honey

1 tbsp chopped fresh mint

2 tbsp chopped fresh coriander

salt and pepper

Preparation time: 15 minutes, plus standing
Cooking time: 15–20 minutes

Each serving provides ⓥ

kcal 249, protein 6 g, fat 7 g (of which saturated fat 0.5 g), carbohydrate 40 g (of which sugars 6 g), fibre 2 g

✓✓ E

✓ copper

1 Heat the oil in a large saucepan, add the almonds and cook gently for 2–3 minutes or until golden. Remove from the pan with a draining spoon and set aside.

2 Add the rice to the oil and cook, stirring, for 1 minute. Stir in the saffron and cinnamon stick, then add the stock and season with salt and pepper to taste. Bring to the boil. Stir, then cover and cook over a very low heat for 10–15 minutes or until the rice is tender and the stock has been absorbed.

3 Meanwhile, cut the pomegranate in half and remove all the seeds from the membranes. Reserve about one-third of the seeds for garnish. Put the rest of the seeds in a sieve placed over a mixing bowl and crush with a spoon to extract the juice.

4 Put the grated ginger into a garlic crusher, hold over the mixing bowl and squeeze out the ginger juice. Stir the honey into the juices.

5 When the rice is cooked, stir in the pomegranate juice mixture. Cover again and leave to stand for 2 minutes. Then remove the cinnamon stick, fork the mint and coriander through the rice, and transfer to a warmed serving dish. Scatter over the almonds and reserved pomegranate seeds, and serve.

Some more ideas

• For lemongrass-scented basmati rice, add a bruised stalk of lemongrass with the cinnamon stick. Instead of pomegranate and ginger juices, mix the juice of ½ lemon with the honey.

• Make a spiced basmati pilaf. Gently cook 55 g (2 oz) cashew nuts in 1 tbsp sunflower oil until golden. Remove from the pan with a draining spoon and set aside. Toast the basmati rice in the oil with 1 tsp cumin seeds and the crushed seeds of 3 cardamom pods for about 2 minutes. Stir in the stock, 3 tbsp coconut milk, 1 bay leaf and 3 cloves. Cover and cook as in the main recipe. Remove the bay leaf and cloves, then stir in 1 tbsp lemon juice and 2 tbsp chopped fresh coriander. Scatter over the cashew nuts and garnish with a sprig of fresh coriander before serving.

Plus points

• Pomegranate seeds not only add flavour to this dish, they also contribute vitamin C and some dietary fibre.

• Almonds, like other nuts, provide many of the nutrients usually found in meat, such as protein, many of the B vitamins and essential minerals such as phosphorus, iron, copper and potassium. They are also a good source of vitamin E, which helps to protect against heart disease.

Chickpea and rice balls

These tasty chickpea-based balls, flavoured with garlic, chilli and lots of fresh coriander, make a delicious alternative to boiled rice or potatoes. They go especially well with Indian food and other spicy dishes.

Serves 4 (makes 12)

100 g (3½ oz) long-grain white rice
1 tbsp sunflower oil
1 small onion, finely chopped
1 garlic clove, crushed
1 fresh red chilli, seeded and finely chopped
2 tomatoes, skinned, seeded and very finely chopped
1 can chickpeas, about 410 g, drained and rinsed
1 egg yolk
3 tbsp chopped fresh coriander
½ tsp paprika
salt and pepper

Preparation time: 50 minutes
Cooking time: 30 minutes

Each serving provides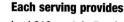

kcal 213, **protein** 7 g, **fat** 6 g (of which saturated fat 1 g), **carbohydrate** 34 g (of which sugars 2.5 g), **fibre** 3 g

✓✓	E
✓	B₁₂, C, iron, zinc

1 Put the rice in a saucepan, add 240 ml (8 fl oz) water and bring to the boil. Cover and simmer very gently for 10–15 minutes or until the rice is tender and has absorbed all the water. Remove from the heat and leave to cool for a few minutes.

2 Meanwhile, preheat the oven to 180°C (350°F, gas mark 4). Heat the oil in a saucepan, add the onion and fry gently for about 5 minutes, stirring frequently, until soft. Stir in the garlic and chilli, and cook for 2 more minutes. Remove from the heat and stir in the chopped tomatoes.

3 Put the chickpeas in a bowl and mash with a potato masher until fairly smooth, or purée them in a food processor. Add the onion mixture, rice, egg yolk, coriander, paprika, and salt and pepper to taste. Mix well. Divide the mixture into 12 equal portions and shape each into a ball.

4 Place the chickpea and rice balls on a greased baking sheet and bake for 30 minutes or until beginning to brown, turning them over carefully halfway through the cooking. Serve hot.

Some more ideas

• Vary the fresh herb according to the food you're serving with the chickpea and rice balls: mint with lamb, or sage and parsley with pork, for example.

• To make onion and chickpea bhajia, gently cook 1 large sliced onion in 1 tbsp sunflower oil for 10 minutes or until very soft. Sift 85 g (3 oz) chickpea (gram) flour into a bowl with 1 tsp ground coriander, 1 tsp turmeric, ½ tsp mild chilli powder and ½ tsp salt. Stir in ½ tsp cumin seeds and make a well in the centre. Add 4 tbsp plain low-fat yogurt, 3 tbsp cold water and 1 tsp lemon juice, and mix to a thick, smooth batter. Stir in the onion and 1 can chickpeas, about 410 g, drained, rinsed and lightly mashed. Heat 1 tbsp sunflower oil in a large non-stick frying pan, drop in spoonfuls of the batter and flatten them slightly with the back of the spoon. Cook over a moderate heat for 2–3 minutes on each side or until dark golden brown and crisp. Drain on kitchen paper and serve hot.

Plus points

• Eating onions regularly can have several beneficial effects, particularly in helping to reduce blood cholesterol levels and lessen the risk of blood clots forming.

• Garlic contains a phytochemical called allicin, which has both anti-fungal and antibiotic properties. For this reason, garlic is thought to help clear cold symptoms and chest infections.

side dishes

Green coriander rice

Making a herb and vegetable paste is a quick and simple way of producing vibrantly coloured, flavoursome rice. Toasting the rice in just a little oil and butter, then cooking with the paste before adding stock and simmering, develops and enriches the flavour of the dish. This makes a great accompaniment to grilled or roast chicken.

Serves 4

1 large green pepper, quartered and seeded

1 onion, quartered

1 garlic clove, crushed

15 g (½ oz) fresh coriander

10 g (scant ½ oz) fresh flat-leaf parsley

10 g (scant ½ oz) butter

2 tsp extra virgin olive oil

225 g (8 oz) long-grain white rice

600 ml (1 pint) boiling chicken stock

salt and pepper

sprigs of fresh coriander to garnish

Preparation time: 15–20 minutes, plus standing
Cooking time: 15–20 minutes

1 Put the green pepper, onion, garlic, coriander and parsley in a food processor and blend to a very finely chopped paste. Alternatively, very finely chop them all together with a knife.

2 Heat the butter and olive oil in a large saucepan, add the rice and fry gently for 2–3 minutes or until the grains are translucent.

3 Remove from the heat and stir in the herb paste. Return to the heat and cook for 2 minutes, stirring all the time. Pour in the boiling stock, and season with salt and pepper to taste. Bring to the boil, then reduce the heat, cover and cook very gently for 10–15 minutes or until the rice is tender and the stock has been absorbed.

4 Remove from the heat and leave to stand, with the pan still covered, for 3–4 minutes. Then fork through to separate the grains. Serve hot, garnished with coriander sprigs.

until tender. About 10 minutes before the rice is ready, gently cook 1 bunch sliced spring onions and 1 crushed garlic clove in 1 tbsp extra virgin olive oil for 3 minutes or until tender. Add 170 g (6 oz) baby spinach leaves, cover and cook for 1 minute, then remove the lid and cook over a low heat for a further minute or until some of the spinach juices have evaporated. Stir in the cooked rice, 3 tbsp chopped parsley, a pinch of freshly grated nutmeg and pepper to taste. Cover and heat through for 2 minutes. Squeeze over the juice of ½ lime, fork through to mix and serve hot.

● To make this a vegetarian dish, use vegetable stock in place of the chicken stock.

Each serving provides

kcal 258, **protein** 5 g, **fat** 4 g (of which saturated fat 1.5 g), **carbohydrate** 53 g (of which sugars 3 g), **fibre** 2 g

✓✓✓ C

✓ A, B$_6$, folate, copper, selenium, zinc

Some more ideas

● Use long-grain brown rice instead of white rice. It will take 30–40 minutes to cook and will need about 100 ml (3½ fl oz) more stock.

● For a spinach and red rice pilaf, cook 225 g (8 oz) Camargue red rice in the butter and oil for 2 minutes, then add 300 ml (10 fl oz) boiling stock. Cook, covered, for 30–35 minutes or

Plus points

● Green peppers are an excellent source of vitamin C, important for maintaining the body's immune system. Even though some of the vitamin C is destroyed during cooking, useful amounts still remain.

● Coriander has over the centuries had many uses other than as a herb in cooking – as an ingredient in liqueur and cologne, as a herbal tonic for the stomach and, with its seeds, for relief of urinary tract problems.

side dishes

Japanese red rice

Red aduki beans give this Japanese rice dish an appealing rosy tint, yet the flavour is mild and creamy. It's an interesting dish to try, particularly if you are experimenting with an Oriental menu.

Serves 4

100 g (3½ oz) dried aduki beans, soaked for at least 8 hours
200 g (7 oz) glutinous rice
½ tsp salt
2 tbsp black sesame seeds

Preparation time: about 1 hour, plus 9 hours soaking and 30 minutes cooling
Cooking time: 25 minutes

1 Drain the soaked beans and rinse under cold running water. Put them into a saucepan, cover with plenty of cold water and bring to the boil. Boil rapidly for 10 minutes, then reduce the heat and simmer for 35–45 minutes or until very tender.

2 Drain the beans in a colander set over a large bowl, reserving the red cooking liquid in the bowl. Leave the liquid to cool for about 30 minutes.

3 Rinse the rice under cold running water until the water is clear, then drain. Add the rice to the red cooking liquid and leave to soak for 1 hour.

4 Drain the rice, saving the red liquid as before. Mix the rice with the cooked beans and measure into a large saucepan, using a measuring jug or a mug. Add an equal quantity of the red liquid, topping up with fresh cold water if needed. Stir in the salt.

5 Bring to the boil. Stir once, then reduce the heat to low and cook very gently for about 15 minutes or until almost all the liquid has been absorbed. Stir again, then cover the pan tightly and turn the heat down to its lowest setting. Leave to steam undisturbed for 10 minutes.

6 Transfer the rice mixture to a serving bowl and use a fork to break it up. Scatter over the sesame seeds and serve.

Another idea
● To make chestnut rice with sake, rinse 225 g (8 oz) Japanese sushi rice, then soak in plenty of cold water for 30 minutes. Drain and put into a large saucepan with 170 g (6 oz) roughly chopped canned or vacuum-packed chestnuts and ½ tsp salt. Add 600 ml (1 pint) cold water. Bring to the boil, then reduce the heat and simmer for 15 minutes or until almost all the liquid has been absorbed, stirring once. Cover tightly and cook, undisturbed, over the lowest possible heat for 10 minutes. Remove from the heat and leave to stand, still covered, for 5 minutes. Remove the lid and fork through the rice, then fork in 1 tbsp sake. Serve sprinkled with 2 tbsp toasted sesame seeds.

Plus points
● Aduki beans are a nutritious addition to savoury dishes of all kinds. In Japan, they are also ground to a powder and used in cakes, pastry and breads, as they have an unusual sweet flavour.
● Combining beans and rice provides a dish rich in starchy carbohydrate and protein, but with a low fat content.
● Sesame seeds can be an important source of protein for vegetarians. They also provide good amounts of calcium, a mineral essential for healthy teeth and bones.

Each serving provides Ⓥ
kcal 283, **protein** 10 g, **fat** 4 g (of which saturated fat 0.5 g), **carbohydrate** 50 g (of which sugars 0.5 g), **fibre** 3 g

✓✓	copper, zinc
✓	B₁, niacin, iron, potassium

side dishes

Boston baked beans

These oven-baked beans are cooked slowly to create a richly flavoured vegetable dish – a revelation if you've only ever eaten the canned variety. Serve alongside grilled meat, together with potatoes or bread.

Serves 6

225 g (8 oz) dried haricot beans, soaked for
    at least 8 hours
1 tbsp sunflower oil
5 shallots, finely chopped
2 garlic cloves, crushed
2 celery sticks, finely chopped
1 can chopped tomatoes, about 400 g
1 can chopped tomatoes, about 225 g
2 tsp dried mixed herbs
500 ml (17 fl oz) dry cider
30 g (1 oz) dark muscovado sugar
1 tbsp black treacle
1 tsp Dijon mustard
salt and pepper
sprigs of fresh flat-leaf parsley to garnish

Preparation time: 1–1½ hours, plus 8 hours
    soaking
Cooking time: 3½ hours

1 Drain the soaked beans and rinse under cold running water. Put them in a saucepan, cover with plenty of fresh cold water and bring to the boil. Boil rapidly for 10 minutes, then reduce the heat and simmer for 50–60 minutes or until tender. Drain well and place in a beanpot or casserole dish.

2 Preheat the oven to 160ºC (325ºF, gas mark 3). Heat the oil in a saucepan, add the shallots, garlic and celery, and sauté for about 5 minutes or until softened, stirring occasionally.

3 Stir in all the canned tomatoes with their juice, the dried herbs, cider, and salt and pepper to taste. Cover and bring to the boil, then reduce the heat and simmer for 10 minutes, stirring occasionally.

4 Add the sugar, treacle and mustard to the tomato sauce, and mix well. Pour the sauce over the beans and stir to mix. Cover the beanpot or casserole and bake for 3½ hours, stirring occasionally. Serve the beans hot, garnished with flat-leaf parsley.

Some more ideas
- Use dry white wine or a well-flavoured vegetable stock instead of cider.
- Instead of haricot beans, try other dried beans, such as black-eyed or cannellini beans.
- For a spicier result, replace the herbs with chilli powder, using mild or hot.

- Make Boston baked lentils. Cook 225 g (8 oz) green or brown lentils in boiling water for about 20 minutes or until tender, then drain well. Make the tomato sauce as in the main recipe, but replacing the shallots with 1 large onion and adding a 2.5 cm (1 in) piece of fresh root ginger, finely chopped, with the garlic. Instead of cider, use 200 ml (7 fl oz) red wine, and omit the mustard. Mix the cooked lentils with the tomato sauce in an ovenproof dish, cover and bake in a preheated 180ºC (350ºF, gas mark 4) oven for 1–1¼ hours.

Plus points
- Shallots tend to have a milder, more subtle flavour than onions, but like onions they contain some vitamin C and B vitamins.
- Unrefined sugars such as muscovado retain a proportion of molasses – the brown residue that contains the nutrients of the sugar cane. In general, the darker the sugar, the more molasses it contains, and the more nutrients.
- Treacle is a sticky fluid refined from molasses. Though it is primarily carbohydrate in the form of sugar, black treacle can provide useful amounts of potassium, calcium and iron.

Each serving provides Ⓥ
kcal 206, protein 9 g, fat 3 g (of which saturated fat 0.5 g), **carbohydrate 33 g** (of which sugars 15 g), **fibre 7 g**

✓✓	copper
✓	B₁, B₆, C, E, niacin, calcium, iron, potassium, zinc

side dishes

Dal with cauliflower and carrots

Dal is one of the staples of Indian cooking. Traditionally it has a sauce-like consistency, but here chunky vegetables have been added to turn it into a more substantial dish – ideal as part of a vegetarian meal. You can vary the vegetables as you wish, as long as they are cut up quite small so that they cook quickly.

Serves 4

2 tbsp sunflower oil

1 onion, chopped

1 large garlic clove, finely chopped

30 g (1 oz) fresh root ginger, finely chopped

200 g (7 oz) yellow lentils

550 ml (18 fl oz) vegetable stock

100 g (3½ oz) carrots, cut into small sticks

170 g (6 oz) cauliflower, cut into small florets

3 tbsp chopped fresh coriander

1 tbsp lemon juice

salt and pepper

Preparation time: 15 minutes

Cooking time: about 45 minutes

1 Heat the oil in a saucepan over a moderate heat, add the onion and garlic, and cook, stirring occasionally, for about 5 minutes or until just starting to soften. Stir in the ginger and cook for a further 3 minutes.

2 Add the lentils and stir to coat with the onion mixture. Pour in the stock, then cover the pan and bring to the boil. Reduce the heat and simmer for about 15 minutes.

3 Add the carrots and cauliflower. Cover the pan again and simmer for 12–15 minutes or until the lentils are tender and the vegetables are cooked.

4 Season with salt and pepper to taste. Stir in the coriander and lemon juice, and serve immediately.

Another idea

• To make spicy split pea dal, sauté the onion, garlic and ginger in the oil as in the main recipe, adding 1 tbsp mild to medium curry powder (depending on your taste) and 1 small fresh red chilli, seeded and finely chopped, with the ginger. Add 200 g (7 oz) yellow split peas with 200 g (7 oz) new potatoes, peeled and cut into dice. Stir, then pour in 750 ml (1¼ pints) vegetable stock and bring to the boil. Cover and simmer for 40–45 minutes or until the split peas are tender. Just before serving, stir in 2 finely chopped tomatoes and 3 tbsp plain low-fat yogurt, and season to taste.

Plus points

• Unlike most vegetables, which are more nutritious when eaten raw, the nutritional value of carrots increases when they are cooked.

• Cauliflower is a member of the brassica family of cruciferous vegetables. It provides useful amounts of vitamin C and dietary fibre and also contains sulphurous compounds thought to help protect against cancer.

Each serving provides Ⓥ

kcal 240, **protein** 15 g, **fat** 7 g (of which saturated fat 1 g), **carbohydrate** 32 g (of which sugars 6 g), **fibre** 6 g

✓✓✓	A, selenium
✓✓	B₆, C, E, copper, iron, zinc
✓	B₁, folate, niacin, potassium

side dishes

Millet with spinach and pine nuts

Bright green spinach and golden apricots add rich colour and flavour to this easy grain and vegetable side dish. Serve it instead of potatoes or rice, with stews and casseroles that have plenty of sauce.

Serves 4

200 g (7 oz) millet

50 g (1¾ oz) ready-to eat dried apricots, roughly chopped

900 ml (1½ pints) vegetable stock

55 g (2 oz) pine nuts

250 g (8½ oz) baby spinach leaves

juice of ½ lemon

salt and pepper

Preparation time: 10 minutes

Cooking time: 20–25 minutes

1 Put the millet and dried apricots into a large saucepan and stir in the stock. Bring to the boil, then lower the heat. Simmer for 15–20 minutes or until all the stock has been absorbed and the millet is tender.

2 Meanwhile, toast the pine nuts in a small frying pan until they are golden brown and fragrant. Set aside.

3 Add the spinach and lemon juice to the millet, with salt and pepper to taste. Cover the pan and leave over a very low heat for 4–5 minutes to wilt the spinach.

4 Stir the millet and spinach mixture gently, then spoon into a serving bowl. Scatter the toasted pine nuts on top and serve immediately.

Another idea

● Try aubergine with millet and sesame seeds. Cut 2 medium-sized aubergines into dice. Heat 2 tbsp extra virgin olive oil in a large frying pan, add the aubergine and brown over a high heat, stirring constantly. Remove from the heat and stir in 200 g (7 oz) millet and 900 ml (1½ pints) vegetable stock. Return to the heat and bring to the boil. Stir, then reduce the heat and simmer for 15–20 minutes or until the stock has been absorbed and the millet is tender. Season with salt and pepper to taste. Transfer to a serving bowl and scatter over 2 tbsp chopped fresh coriander, 1 tbsp thinly sliced spring onions and 2 tbsp toasted sesame seeds.

Plus points

● Millet provides useful amounts of iron and B vitamins and, as it is not highly milled, it retains all its nutritional value. Being gluten-free, it can be an additional source of starchy carbohydrate for coeliacs.

● Pine nuts are a good source of vitamin E and potassium. They also contribute useful amounts of magnesium, zinc and iron.

● Dried apricots are one of the richest fruit sources of iron. They also contain beta-carotene, which the body can convert to vitamin A, and other minerals such as calcium, potassium and phosphorus.

Each serving provides Ⓥ

kcal 307, **protein** 7 g, **fat** 11 g (of which saturated fat 1 g), **carbohydrate** 44 g (of which sugars 6 g), **fibre** 2 g

✓✓✓	A
✓✓	B₁, E
✓	C, folate, niacin, calcium, copper, iron, potassium, zinc

side dishes

152

Cajun barley

Barley is one of the crops that farmers love, due to its short growing season and hardy nature. We should love this nutty, wholesome grain too, since it is so good for us. Here it has been given the flavours of the American Deep South, with a range of green vegetables and plenty of spice. Serve it with sausages or lamb kebabs.

Serves 4

200 g (7 oz) pearl barley
2 tbsp extra virgin olive oil
4 spring onions, the white and green parts chopped separately
2 celery sticks, chopped
1 onion, chopped
1 green pepper, seeded and chopped
1 fresh green chilli, seeded and finely chopped
2 garlic cloves, finely chopped
½ tsp ground cumin
¼ tsp dried thyme
¼ tsp cracked black peppercorns
pinch of cayenne pepper
500 ml (17 fl oz) vegetable stock
2 tbsp lemon juice
salt
lemon wedges to serve

Preparation time: 15 minutes
Cooking time: 40–50 minutes

Each serving provides Ⓥ

kcal 255, protein 5 g, fat 7 g (of which saturated fat 1 g), carbohydrate 47 g (of which sugars 4 g), fibre 2 g

✓✓✓ C

✓ B_6, folate, niacin, copper, iron, zinc

1 Heat a heavy-based frying pan over a moderate heat. Add the pearl barley and toast, stirring constantly, for about 4 minutes or until the grains just start to brown and smell fragrant. Remove from the heat immediately, transfer to a shallow bowl and set aside.

2 Heat the oil in a flameproof casserole over a moderate heat. Add the white parts of the spring onions, the celery, onion and green pepper, and sauté for about 5 minutes or until slightly softened, stirring occasionally.

3 Stir in the chilli, garlic, cumin, thyme, peppercorns and cayenne pepper. Sauté for a further 5 minutes, stirring well.

4 Add the barley and stock to the casserole. Bring to the boil, then cover, reduce the heat and simmer for 30–40 minutes or until the barley is tender and the liquid has been absorbed.

5 Season with salt to taste and stir in the lemon juice. Scatter over the green spring onion tops and serve, with lemon wedges.

Some more ideas

• For Tex-Mex barley, omit the celery, green pepper and thyme, and add 1 finely chopped fresh red chilli and the finely grated zest of 1 lime in step 3. Add the juice of the lime in place of the lemon juice.

• To make braised barley, omit the toasting of the barley, but cook the spring onions, celery, onion and green pepper as in the main recipe. Add ¼ tsp each of dried thyme and sage, ¼ tsp ground cumin and a pinch of cayenne pepper, and sauté for 5 more minutes. Add the pearl barley and stock, and cook as in the main recipe. About 10 minutes before the barley is done, add 100 g (3½ oz) small broccoli florets and 100 g (3½ oz) green beans, cut into 2 cm (¾ in) pieces. Before serving, stir in 1 tbsp snipped fresh chives.

Plus points

• Barley has a similar nutrient content to other cereals, with most of the minerals and vitamins in the outer layers. When the outer bran and germ are removed to make pearl barley, there is some loss of vitamins, particularly B_1.

• Extra virgin olive oil is made from the first pressing of top grade olives. Because it is produced with minimal heat and refining, it retains more phytochemicals and essential fatty acids than highly refined oils.

• Weight for weight, chillies are richer in vitamin C than citrus fruits such as oranges. However, to gain this nutritional benefit you would have to eat substantially more chillies than you are likely to, or would want, to eat.

A glossary of nutritional terms

Antioxidants These are compounds that help to protect the body's cells against the damaging effects of free radicals. Vitamins C and E, beta-carotene (the plant form of vitamin A) and the mineral selenium, together with many of the phytochemicals found in fruit and vegetables, all act as antioxidants.

Calorie A unit used to measure the energy value of food and the intake and use of energy by the body. The scientific definition of 1 calorie is the amount of heat required to raise the temperature of 1 gram of water by 1 degree Centigrade. This is such a small amount that in this country we tend to use the term kilocalories (abbreviated to *kcal*), which is equivalent to 1000 calories. Energy values can also be measured in kilojoules (kJ): 1 kcal = 4.2 kJ.

A person's energy (calorie) requirement varies depending on his or her age, sex and level of activity. The estimated average daily energy requirements are:

Age (years)	Female (kcal)	Male (kcal)
1–3	1165	1230
4–6	1545	1715
7–10	1740	1970
11–14	1845	2220
15–18	2110	2755
19–49	1940	2550
50–59	1900	2550
60–64	1900	2380
65–74	1900	2330

Carbohydrates These energy-providing substances are present in varying amounts in different foods and are found in three main forms: sugars, starches and non-starch polysaccharides (NSP), usually called fibre.

There are two types of sugars: *intrinsic sugars*, which occur naturally in fruit (fructose) and sweet-tasting vegetables, and *extrinsic sugars*, which include lactose (from milk) and all the non-milk extrinsic sugars (NMEs) – sucrose (table sugar), honey, treacle, molasses and so on. The NMEs, or 'added' sugars, provide only calories, whereas foods containing intrinsic sugars also offer vitamins, minerals and fibre. Added sugars (*simple carbohydrates*) are digested and absorbed rapidly to provide energy very quickly. Starches and fibre (*complex carbohydrates*), on the other hand, break down more slowly to offer a longer-term energy source (see also Glycaemic Index). Starchy carbohydrates are found in bread, pasta, rice, wholegrain and breakfast cereals, and potatoes and other starchy vegetables such as parsnips, sweet potatoes and yams.

Healthy eating guidelines recommend that at least half of our daily energy (calories) should come from carbohydrates, and that most of this should be from complex carbohydrates. No more than 11% of our total calorie intake should come from 'added' sugars. For an average woman aged 19–49 years, this would mean a total carbohydrate intake of 259 g per day, of which 202 g should be from starch and intrinsic sugars and no more than 57 g from added sugars. For a man of the same age, total carbohydrates each day should be about 340 g (265 g from starch and intrinsic sugars and 75 g from added sugars).

See also Fibre and Glycogen.

Cholesterol There are two types of cholesterol – the soft waxy substance called blood cholesterol, which is an integral part of human cell membranes, and dietary cholesterol, which is contained in food. *Blood cholesterol* is important in the formation of some hormones and it aids digestion. High blood cholesterol levels are known to be an important risk factor for coronary heart disease, but most of the cholesterol in our blood is made by the liver – only about 25% comes from cholesterol in food. So while it would seem that the amount of cholesterol-rich foods in the diet would have a direct effect on blood cholesterol levels, in fact the best way to reduce blood cholesterol is to eat less saturated fat and to increase intake of foods containing soluble fibre.

Fat Although a small amount of fat is essential for good health, most people consume far too much. Healthy eating guidelines recommend that no more than 33% of our daily energy intake (calories) should come from fat. Each gram of fat contains 9 kcal, more than twice as many calories as carbohydrate or protein, so for a woman aged 19–49 years this means a daily maximum of 71 g fat, and for a man in the same age range 93.5 g fat.

Fats can be divided into 3 main groups: saturated, monounsaturated and polyunsaturated, depending on the chemical structure of the fatty acids they contain. *Saturated fatty acids* are found mainly in animal fats such as butter and other dairy products and in fatty meat. A high intake of saturated fat is known to be a risk factor for coronary heart disease and certain types of cancer. Current guidelines are that no more than 10% of our daily calories should come from saturated fats, which is about 21.5 g for an adult woman and 28.5 g for a man.

Where saturated fats tend to be solid at room temperature, the *unsaturated fatty acids* –

monounsaturated and polyunsaturated – tend to be liquid. *Monounsaturated fats* are found predominantly in olive oil, groundnut (peanut) oil, rapeseed oil and avocados. Foods high in *polyunsaturates* include most vegetable oils – the exceptions are palm oil and coconut oil, both of which are saturated.

Both saturated and monounsaturated fatty acids can be made by the body, but certain polyunsaturated fatty acids – known as *essential fatty acids* – must be supplied by food. There are 2 'families' of these essential fatty acids: *omega-6*, derived from linoleic acid, and *omega-3*, from linolenic acid. The main food sources of the omega-6 family are vegetable oils such as olive and sunflower; omega-3 fatty acids are provided by oily fish, nuts, and vegetable oils such as soya and rapeseed.

When vegetable oils are hydrogenated (hardened) to make margarine and reduced-fat spreads, their unsaturated fatty acids can be changed into trans fatty acids, or '*trans fats*'. These artificially produced trans fats are believed to act in the same way as saturated fats within the body – with the same risks to health. Current healthy eating guidelines suggest that no more than 2% of our daily calories should come from trans fats, which is about 4.3 g for an adult woman and 5.6 g for a man. In thinking about the amount of trans fats you consume, remember that major sources are processed foods such as biscuits, pies, cakes and crisps.

Fibre Technically non-starch polysaccharides (NSP), fibre is the term commonly used to describe several different compounds, such as pectin, hemicellulose, lignin and gums, which are found in the cell walls of all plants. The body cannot digest fibre, nor does it have much nutritional value, but it plays an important role in helping us to stay healthy.

Fibre can be divided into 2 groups – soluble and insoluble. Both types are provided by most plant foods, but some foods are particularly good sources of one type or the other. *Soluble fibre* (in oats, pulses, fruit and vegetables) can help to reduce high blood cholesterol levels and to control blood sugar levels by slowing down the absorption of sugar. *Insoluble fibre* (in wholegrain cereals, pulses, fruit and vegetables) increases stool bulk and speeds the passage of waste material through the body. In this way it helps to prevent constipation, haemorrhoids and diverticular disease, and may protect against bowel cancer.

Our current intake of fibre is around 12 g a day. Healthy eating guidelines suggest that we need to increase this amount to 18 g a day.

Free radicals These highly reactive molecules can cause damage to cell walls and DNA (the genetic material found within cells). They are believed to be involved in the development of heart disease, some cancers and premature ageing. Free radicals are produced naturally by the body in the course of everyday life, but certain factors, such as cigarette smoke, pollution and over-exposure to sunlight, can accelerate their production.

Gluten A protein found in wheat and, to a lesser degree, in rye, barley and oats, but not in corn (maize) or rice. People with *coeliac disease* have a sensitivity to gluten and need to eliminate all gluten-containing foods, such as bread, pasta, cakes and biscuits, from their diet.

Glycaemic Index (GI) This is used to measure the rate at which carbohydrate foods are digested and converted into sugar (glucose) to raise blood sugar levels and provide energy. Foods with a high GI are quickly broken down and offer an immediate energy fix, while those with a lower GI are absorbed more slowly, making you feel full for longer and helping to keep blood sugar levels constant. High-GI foods include table sugar, honey, mashed potatoes and watermelon. Low-GI foods include pulses, wholewheat cereals, apples, cherries, dried apricots, pasta and oats.

Glycogen This is one of the 2 forms in which energy from carbohydrates is made available for use by the body (the other is *glucose*). Whereas glucose is converted quickly from carbohydrates and made available in the blood for a fast energy fix, glycogen is stored in the liver and muscles to fuel longer-term energy needs. When the body has used up its immediate supply of glucose, the stored glycogen is broken down into glucose to continue supplying energy.

Minerals These inorganic substances perform a wide range of vital functions in the body. The *macrominerals* – calcium, chloride, magnesium, potassium, phosphorus and sodium – are needed in relatively large quantities, whereas much smaller amounts are required of the remainder, called *microminerals*. Some microminerals (selenium, magnesium and iodine, for example) are needed in such tiny amounts that they are known as *'trace elements'*.

There are important differences in the body's ability to absorb minerals from different foods, and this can be affected by the presence of other substances. For example, oxalic acid, present in spinach, interferes with the absorption of much of the iron and calcium spinach contains.
• *Calcium* is essential for the development of strong bones and teeth. It also plays an important role in blood clotting. Good sources include dairy products, canned fish (eaten with their bones) and dark green, leafy vegetables.
• *Chloride* helps to maintain the body's fluid balance. The main source in the diet is table salt.
• *Chromium* is important in the regulation of blood sugar levels, as well as levels of fat and cholesterol in the blood. Good dietary sources include red meat, liver, eggs, seafood, cheese and wholegrain cereals.

• *Copper*, component of many enzymes, is needed for bone growth and the formation of connective tissue. It helps the body to absorb iron from food. Good sources include offal, shellfish, mushrooms, cocoa, nuts and seeds.
• *Iodine* is an important component of the thyroid hormones, which govern the rate and efficiency at which food is converted into energy. Good sources include seafood, seaweed and vegetables (depending on the iodine content of the soil in which they are grown).
• *Iron* is an essential component of haemoglobin, the pigment in red blood cells that carries oxygen around the body. Good sources are offal, red meat, dried apricots and prunes, and iron-fortified breakfast cereals.
• *Magnesium* is important for healthy bones, the release of energy from food, and nerve and muscle function. Good sources include wholegrain cereals, peas and other green vegetables, pulses, dried fruit and nuts.
• *Manganese* is a vital component of several enzymes that are involved in energy production and many other functions. Good dietary sources include nuts, cereals, brown rice, pulses and wholemeal bread.
• *Molybdenum* is an essential component of several enzymes, including those involved in the production of DNA. Good sources are offal, yeast, pulses, wholegrain cereals and green leafy vegetables.
• *Phosphorus* is important for healthy bones and teeth and for the release of energy from foods. It is found in most foods. Particularly good sources include dairy products, red meat, poultry, fish and eggs.
• *Potassium*, along with sodium, is important in maintaining fluid balance and regulating blood pressure, and is essential for the transmission of nerve impulses. Good sources include fruit, especially bananas and citrus fruits, nuts, seeds, potatoes and pulses.
• *Selenium* is a powerful antioxidant that protects cells against damage by free radicals. Good dietary sources are meat, fish, dairy foods, brazil nuts, avocados and lentils.
• *Sodium* works with potassium to regulate fluid balance, and is essential for nerve and muscle function. Only a little sodium is needed – we tend to get too much in our diet. The main source in the diet is table salt, as well as salty processed foods and ready-prepared foods.
• *Sulphur* is a component of 2 essential amino acids. Protein foods are the main source.
• *Zinc* is vital for normal growth, as well as reproduction and immunity. Good dietary sources include oysters, red meat, peanuts and sunflower seeds.

Phytochemicals These biologically active compounds, found in most plant foods, are believed to be beneficial in disease prevention. There are literally thousands of different phytochemicals, amongst which are the following:

• *Allicin*, a phytochemical found in garlic, onions, leeks, chives and shallots, is believed to help lower high blood cholesterol levels and stimulate the immune system.
• *Bioflavonoids*, of which there are at least 6000, are found mainly in fruit and sweet-tasting vegetables. Different bioflavonoids have different roles – some are antioxidants, while others act as anti-disease agents. A sub-group of these phytochemicals, called *flavonols*, includes the antioxidant *quercetin*, which is believed to reduce the risk of heart disease and help to protect against cataracts. Quercetin is found in tea, red wine, grapes and broad beans.
• *Carotenoids*, the best known of which are *beta-carotene* and *lycopene*, are powerful antioxidants thought to help protect us against certain types of cancer. Highly coloured fruits and vegetables, such as blackcurrants, mangoes, tomatoes, carrots, sweet potatoes, pumpkin and dark green, leafy vegetables, are excellent sources of carotenoids.
• *Coumarins* are believed to help protect against cancer by inhibiting the formation of tumours. Oranges are a rich source.
• *Glucosinolates*, found mainly in cruciferous vegetables, particularly broccoli, Brussels sprouts, cabbage, kale and cauliflower, are believed to have strong anti-cancer effects. *Sulphoraphane* is one of the powerful cancer-fighting substances produced by glucosinolates.
• *Phytoestrogens* have a chemical structure similar to the female hormone oestrogen, and they are believed to help protect against hormone-related cancers such as breast and prostate cancer. One of the types of these phytochemicals, called *isoflavones*, may also help to relieve symptoms associated with the menopause. Soya beans and chickpeas are a particularly rich source of isoflavones.

Protein This nutrient, necessary for growth and development, for maintenance and repair of cells, and for the production of enzymes, antibodies and hormones, is essential to keep the body working efficiently. Protein is made up of *amino acids*, which are compounds containing the 4 elements that are necessary for life: carbon, hydrogen, oxygen and nitrogen. We need all of the 20 amino acids commonly found in plant and animal proteins. The human body can make 12 of these, but the remaining 8 – called *essential amino acids* – must be obtained from the food we eat.

Protein comes in a wide variety of foods. Meat, fish, dairy products, eggs and soya beans contain all of the essential amino acids, and are therefore called first-class protein foods. Pulses, nuts, seeds and cereals are also good sources of protein, but do not contain the full range of essential amino acids. In practical terms, this really doesn't matter – as long as you include a variety of different protein foods in your diet, your body will get all the amino acids it needs. It is important, though, to eat protein foods

glossary

every day because the essential amino acids cannot be stored in the body for later use.

The RNI of protein for women aged 19–49 years is 45 g per day and for men of the same age 55 g. In the UK most people eat more protein than they need, although this isn't normally a problem.

Reference Nutrient Intake (RNI) This denotes the average daily amount of vitamins and minerals thought to be sufficient to meet the nutritional needs of almost all individuals within the population. The figures, published by the Department of Health, vary depending on age, sex and specific nutritional needs such as pregnancy. RNIs are equivalent to what used to be called Recommended Daily Amounts or Allowances (RDA).

RNIs for adults (19–49 years)

Vitamin A	600–700 mcg
Vitamin B_1	0.8 mg for women, 1 mg for men
Vitamin B_2	1.1 mg for women, 1.3 mg for men
Niacin	13 mg for women, 17 mg for men
Vitamin B_6	1.2 mg for women, 1.4 mg for men
Vitamin B_{12}	1.5 mg
Folate	200 mcg (400 mcg for first trimester of pregnancy)
Vitamin C	40 mg
Vitamin E	no recommendation in the UK; the EC RDA is 10 mg, which has been used in all recipe analyses in this book
Calcium	700 mg
Chloride	2500 mg
Copper	1.2 mg
Iodine	140 mcg
Iron	14.8 mg for women, 8.7 mg for men
Magnesium	270–300 mg
Phosphorus	550 mg
Potassium	3500 mg
Selenium	60 mcg for women, 75 mcg for men
Sodium	1600 mg
Zinc	7 mg for women, 9.5 mg for men

Vitamins These are organic compounds that are essential for good health. Although they are required in only small amounts, each one has specific vital functions to perform. Most vitamins cannot be made by the human body, and therefore must be obtained from the diet. The body is capable of storing some vitamins (A, D, E, K and B_{12}), but the rest need to be provided by the diet on a regular basis. A well-balanced diet, containing a wide variety of different foods, is the best way to ensure that you get all the vitamins you need.

Vitamins can be divided into 2 groups: *water-soluble* (B complex and C) and *fat-soluble* (A, D, E and K). Water-soluble vitamins are easily destroyed during processing, storage, and the preparation and cooking of food. The fat-soluble vitamins are less vulnerable to losses during cooking and processing.

• *Vitamin A* (retinol) is essential for healthy vision, eyes, skin and growth. Good sources include dairy products, offal (especially liver), eggs and oily fish. Vitamin A can also be obtained from *beta-carotene*, the pigment found in highly coloured fruit and vegetables. In addition to acting as a source of vitamin A, beta-carotene has an important role to play as an antioxidant in its own right.

• *The B Complex vitamins* have very similar roles to play in nutrition, and many of them occur together in the same foods.

Vitamin B_1 (thiamin) is essential in the release of energy from carbohydrates. Good sources include milk, offal, meat (especially pork), wholegrain and fortified breakfast cereals, nuts and pulses, yeast extract and wheat germ. White flour and bread are fortified with B_1 in the UK.

Vitamin B_2 (riboflavin) is vital for growth, healthy skin and eyes, and the release of energy from food. Good sources include milk, meat, offal, eggs, cheese, fortified breakfast cereals, yeast extract and green leafy vegetables.

Niacin (nicotinic acid), sometimes called vitamin B_3, plays an important role in the release of energy within the cells. Unlike the other B vitamins it can be made by the body from the essential amino acid tryptophan. Good sources include meat, offal, fish, fortified breakfast cereals and pulses. White flour and bread are fortified with niacin in the UK.

Pantothenic acid, sometimes called vitamin B_5, is involved in a number of metabolic reactions, including energy production. This vitamin is present in most foods; notable exceptions are fat, oil and sugar. Good sources include liver, kidneys, yeast, egg yolks, fish roe, wheat germ, nuts, pulses and fresh vegetables.

Vitamin B_6 (pyridoxine) helps the body to utilise protein and contributes to the formation of haemoglobin for red blood cells. B_6 is found in a wide range of foods including meat, liver, fish, eggs, wholegrain cereals, some vegetables, pulses, brown rice, nuts and yeast extract.

Vitamin B_{12} (cyanocobalamin) is vital for growth, the formation of red blood cells and maintenance of a healthy nervous system. B_{12} is unique in that it is principally found in foods of animal origin. Vegetarians who eat dairy products will get enough, but vegans need to ensure they include food fortified with B_{12} in their diet. Good sources of B_{12} include liver, kidneys, oily fish, meat, cheese, eggs and milk.

Folate (folic acid) is involved in the manufacture of amino acids and in the production of red blood cells. Recent research suggests that folate may also help to protect against heart disease. Good sources of folate are green leafy vegetables, liver, pulses, eggs, wholegrain cereal products and fortified breakfast cereals, brewers' yeast, wheatgerm, nuts and fruit, especially grapefruit and oranges.

Biotin is needed for various metabolic reactions and the release of energy from foods. Good sources include liver, oily fish, brewers' yeast, kidneys, egg yolks and brown rice.

• *Vitamin C* (ascorbic acid) is essential for growth and vital for the formation of collagen (a protein needed for healthy bones, teeth, gums, blood capillaries and all connective tissue). It plays an important role in the healing of wounds and fractures, and acts as a powerful antioxidant. Vitamin C is found mainly in fruit and vegetables.

• *Vitamin D* (cholecalciferol) is essential for growth and the absorption of calcium, and thus for the formation of healthy bones. It is also involved in maintaining a healthy nervous system. The amount of vitamin D occurring naturally in foods is small, and it is found in very few foods – good sources are oily fish (and fish liver oil supplements), eggs and liver, as well as breakfast cereals, margarine and full-fat milk that are fortified with vitamin D. Most vitamin D, however, does not come from the diet but is made by the body when the skin is exposed to sunlight.

• *Vitamin E* is not one vitamin, but a number of related compounds called tocopherols that function as antioxidants. Good sources of vitamin E are vegetable oils, polyunsaturated margarines, wheatgerm, sunflower seeds, nuts, oily fish, eggs, wholegrain cereals, avocados and spinach.

• *Vitamin K* is essential for the production of several proteins, including prothombin which is involved in the clotting of blood. It has been found to exist in 3 forms, one of which is obtained from food while the other 2 are made by the bacteria in the intestine. Vitamin K_1, which is the form found in food, is present in broccoli, cabbage, spinach, milk, margarine, vegetable oils, particularly soya oil, cereals, liver, alfalfa and kelp.

Nutritional analyses

The nutritional analysis of each recipe has been carried out using data from *The Composition of Foods* with additional data from food manufacturers where appropriate. Because the level and availability of different nutrients can vary, depending on factors like growing conditions and breed of animal, the figures are intended as an approximate guide only.

The analyses include vitamins A, B_1, B_2, B_6, B_{12}, niacin, folate, C, D and E, and the minerals calcium, copper, iron, potassium, selenium and zinc. Other vitamins and minerals are not included, as deficiencies are rare. Optional ingredients and optional serving suggestions have not been included in the calculations.

glossary

Index

index

Printing and binding: Tien Wah Press Limited, Singapore
Separations: Colour Systems Ltd, London
Paper: StoraEnso

Book code: 400-200-01
ISBN: 0 276 42889 7
Oracle Code: 250008440S